Contracts in Publishing
A Toolkit for Authors and Publishers

WIPO
WORLD
INTELLECTUAL PROPERTY
ORGANIZATION

Suggested citation: World Intellectual Property Organization (WIPO) *Contracts in publishing: A toolkit for authors and publishers* (2024). *Publication title*. Geneva: WIPO. DOI 10.34667/tind.49376

First published 2024

World Intellectual Property Organization
34, chemin des Colombettes, P.O. Box 18
CH-1211 Geneva 20, Switzerland

wipo.int

ISBN: 978-92-805-3628-7 (print)
ISBN: 978-92-805-3629-4 (online)

Cover:
Getty Images / Shulz, Narvikk Unsplash / Olia Gozha

WIPO Publication No. 2001EN

Contents

Foreword 6

Acknowledgements 7

Acronyms 8

1 Introduction 9

2 What is publishing? 12

2.1 The value chain in summary 12
- 2.1.1 The roles of the main parties 12
- 2.1.2 Licensing 13
- 2.1.3 Self-publishing 13
- 2.1.4 Support for authors 14

2.2 Authors, publishers and authors' rights or copyright 14
- 2.2.1 The history of copyright law 15
- 2.2.2 The scope of copyright 15
- 2.2.3 Reversion of copyright 16
- 2.2.4 Visual creators 16
- 2.2.5 Reproduction and piracy 16
- 2.2.6 Assignment of copyright 17

2.3 The publishing value chain and process 18
- 2.3.1 The origin of a published work 18
- 2.3.2 Added value by the publisher 19
- 2.3.3 Payment 19
- 2.3.4 Translation 19
- 2.3.5 Illustrations and photography 20
- 2.3.6 Re-editioning, distribution and sales 20

2.4 The author's responsibilities 20
- 2.4.1 Joint authorship 21

2.5 The publisher's responsibilities 21
- 2.5.1 Author names 21
- 2.5.2 Payment 21
- 2.5.3 Relevance and demand 22
- 2.5.4 Design 22

2.6 Traditional publishing models 22
- 2.6.1 General, consumer or trade publishing 22
- 2.6.2 Educational and academic publishing 22
- 2.6.3 Professional and specialist publishing 23

2.7 Alternative publishing models 23
- 2.7.1 E-book and digital-first publishing 23
- 2.7.2 Self-publishing, vanity publishing and hybrid publishing 24

2.8 The role of the literary agent 24

2.9 From books to other formats 25

3 Contracts: why and how 26

3.1 The principle of fair contracts and minimum terms agreements 27

3.2 Boilerplate and standard contracts 28

4 Publishing contracts: the nuts and bolts **29**

4.1 The preamble: parties to the contract and brief scope of work **29**
4.2 Effective date, term and earlier agreements **30**
4.3 The grant of rights **30**
4.3.1 Exclusivity and non-exclusivity 31
4.3.2 Language and territory 31
4.3.3 Term of contract: full term of copyright (FTOC) or fixed-term agreements 32
4.3.4 Volume form definition 33
4.3.5 No abridgment or extract agreement 34
4.3.6 Subsequent editions 34

4.4 Author's warranties and indemnities **35**
4.5 Author's reserved rights **35**
4.6 Author's delivery: text length, illustrations, photos, permissions, index **35**
4.7 Publisher's acceptance or decision not to publish **36**
4.8 Editing, author's corrections and proofs **37**
4.9 Publication: time frame, format, design and promotion **37**
4.9.1 Time frame for publication 37
4.9.2 Format: hardback, paperback, e-book, audio 37
4.9.3 Title, cover, description: consultation and approval 37
4.9.4 Author promotion, approved biography and photographs 38
4.9.5 Marketing materials and proposed retail price 38

4.10 Return of manuscript and other materials belonging to the author **38**
4.11 Copyright notice **38**
4.12 Moral rights and changes to the work **39**
4.13 Advance payments **40**
4.13.1 Multiple book deals: separate or joint accounting 41

4.14 Royalties **41**
4.14.1 Hardback 42
4.14.2 Paperback editions: trade and mass market 42
4.14.3 E-book 43
4.14.4 Audio 43
4.14.5 Translator fees or royalties 44
4.14.6 Free or promotional copies 44

4.15 Subsidiary rights **44**
4.15.1 First and second serial rights 45
4.15.2 Editions in other territories 46
4.15.3 Other format editions 46
4.15.4 Translation rights 46
4.15.5 Book club rights 47
4.15.6 Large print rights 47
4.15.7 Free license for visually impaired person access 47
4.15.8 Condensation rights 48
4.15.9 Anthology rights and permissions 48
4.15.10 Educational editions 49
4.15.11 Merchandizing 49
4.15.12 Audio 49
4.15.13 Radio 50
4.15.14 Film, television and theater rights 50
4.15.15 Rental and lending rights 51
4.15.16 Online database rights 52
4.15.17 CD-ROM optical disk rights 52
4.15.18 Digital technology, learning tools and publisher-owned content 52
4.15.19 Collective licensing 53
4.15.20 Supply of subsidiary agreements 55

4.16 Film quit claim **55**
4.17 Accounting: statements, payments, examination and remedies **55**
4.17.1 Statements and payments 55
4.17.2 Examination and remedies 56
4.17.3 Tax note 56

4.18 Author's copies **56**
4.19 Termination: publication cessation, rate of sale, remainders **56**
4.20 Termination: bankruptcy or liquidation **57**
4.21 Copyright infringement **57**
4.22 Force majeure **58**
4.23 Disputes and interpretation **58**
4.24 Applicable or governing law **58**
4.25 Assignment and non-assignment **59**
4.26 Option clauses **59**

4.27 Competing works 60
4.28 Agency clause 60
4.29 Entire and earlier agreements 60
4.30 Signature and contract copies 60

5 After the contract **61**

6 Conclusion **62**

Useful links **63**

Copyright information: principles, permissions, piracy and FAQs for authors 63
Other publishing matters 64
International authors', translators' and artists' associations 64
International publishing organizations and associations 65
International agents' associations 65
Copyright, IP, PLR, collective licensing and related organizations 66
Further on contractual matters, campaigning, fair terms, model contracts 66

Bibliography and further reading resources **67**

Foreword

For many years, WIPO has been instrumental in supporting creators across its Member States, providing them with tools to manage copyright and related rights.

An initiative launched by WIPO in 2018 known as the "Publishers Circle" illustrates this commitment. This public-private partnership aims to promote the transfer of knowledge within the book publishing industry, building skills and raising professional standards on the basis of a sound legal framework, especially in developing countries. The overarching objective of the initiative is to cultivate a robust, globally connected and efficient publishing landscape in all the regions of the world.

It was within the framework of this initiative that WIPO started to develop the Toolkit in 2021, with a specific focus on empowering authors and publishers. The objective is to provide those creators and professionals with a checklist of the most essential considerations while drafting and concluding a contract.

To ensure the creation of a well-balanced resource that meets the needs of both authors and publishers, the task of drafting the content was entrusted to two esteemed individuals: Mr. Brian Wafawarowa, Chairperson of the Publishers Association of South Africa (PASA), and Ms. Isobel Dixon, a renowned South African poet and Head of Books at Blake Friedmann Literary Agency in the UK. The fruition of this publication owes much to the unwavering dedication and invaluable contributions of Brian and Isobel, drawing from their extensive practical experiences over the past few years.

Throughout the development process, stakeholders were consulted to ensure that the Toolkit offers a comprehensive and balanced perspective for its readers. I extend my sincere gratitude to all those involved for their invaluable comments and inputs, including the European Visual Artists (EVA), the European Writers' Council (EWC), the International Authors Forum (IAF), the International Federation of Reproduction Rights Organisations (IFRRO), the International Publishers Association (IPA) and the International Association of Scientific, Technical, and Medical Publishers (STM).

It is my dear hope that this publication will serve as a practical resource for authors and publishers alike; it is especially dedicated to those in the developing world, offering invaluable guidance on key contractual considerations at various stages of the publishing journey.

Sylvie Forbin
Deputy Director General, WIPO

Acknowledgements

Contracts in Publishing: A Toolkit for Authors and Publishers was developed under the general direction of Sylvie Forbin (WIPO Deputy Director General) and Benoît Müller (WIPO Director of Copyright Management Division) and authored by Brian Wafawarowa and Isobel Dixon. Anita Huss-Ekerhult (formerly WIPO Counsellor of Copyright Management Division) and Miyuki Monroig (WIPO Program Officer of Copyright Management Division) implemented the project.

The *Toolkit* benefited greatly from reviews and comments by experts, including Barbara Hayes, Carlo Lavizzari, Carola Streul, Caroline Morgan, José Borghino and Nina George.

Finally, thank you to WIPO editorial and design colleagues in the Publications and Design Section for leading the production of the report .

Acronyms

AG	Authors Guild
AI	artificial intelligence
ALCS	Authors' Licensing and Collecting Society
ANZ	Australia and New Zealand
APNET	African Publishers Network
BBC	British Broadcasting Corporation
BCC	British Copyright Council
CEATL	European Council of Literary Translators' Associations
CMO	collective management organization
DACS	Design and Artists Copyright Society
EU	European Union
EVA	European Visual Artists
EWC	European Writers' Council
FAQ	frequently asked question
FEP	Federation of European Publishers
FTOC	full term of copyright
GST	general sales tax
IAF	International Authors Forum
IFRRO	International Federation of Reproduction Rights Organisations
IP	intellectual property
IPA	International Publishers Association
ISCC	International Standard Content Code
OA	open access
OER	open education resource
PLR	Public Lending Right
POD	print-on-demand
RRO	reproduction rights organization
SOA	Society of Authors
STM	International Association of Scientific, Technical and Medical Publishers
TBMA	to be mutually agreed
TDM	text and data mining
VAT	value added tax
WAL	world all languages
WEL	world English language
WGGB	Writers' Guild of Great Britain
WIPO	World Intellectual Property Organization

1 Introduction

Through a brief overview of the principle of copyright (including authors' rights) legislations and the components of publishing contracts, *Contracts in Publishing: A Toolkit for Authors and Publishers* seeks to offer authors, publishers and their potential agents insights into the operation of the publishing agreement as one of the most important factors for joint work and an amicable relationship. On the basis of organized licensing of protected works, the contract protects and enables the signing parties, ensuring both the author and the publisher are fairly rewarded, along with authors and contributors such as illustrators and translators. The contract is a record of the parties' rights and obligations and serves as clear reference and guide to recourse in the case of any future dispute. It is from this strong, clearly signposted base that publishers (and, where applicable, agents) can set out to be better champions of authors' essential creative output, distributing their works as widely as possible throughout the world.

There is a well-known saying, "It takes a village to raise a child." The same can be said to be true of publishing and the communal efforts involved in the writing, editing, production and dissemination of an author's work – the making of a book. Publishing is a wide-ranging creative and commercial enterprise, shaping original texts for distribution in the many formats through which readers (and listeners) of all ages and backgrounds can learn from informative, educational, non-fiction texts and can enjoy literary works – with "literary" used in its widest sense, covering all narrative genres and poetry. When this toolkit refers to "the book," many different forms of intellectual property (IP), knowledge sharing and narrative delivery in print and digital formats are involved. Similarly, this toolkit will often refer to "the author" in a way that includes writers, translators, illustrators and photographers. Given the range of publishing possibilities, the scope of references will necessarily be broad, addressing general principles, often with more focus on general, educational or trade publishing, though with additional links and material for further consultation on specific areas of interests.

There are significant differences between trade and educational publishing. This toolkit provides an overview of both, although some aspects of the suggested contractual considerations might be more relevant to one approach than another. Generally speaking, in the trade sector, the book tends to be initiated by an author who, through their own unpaid pre-investment (in terms of time, labor, research), puts the work together and approaches a publisher to publish and promote the work. In the education field, publishing work is often triggered by the curriculum and its requirements; publishers commission suitable authors to write and develop the work according to the requirements of the curriculum. The work involves several participants, including illustrators and trainers who test the material among learners. It also involves submission to the education authorities for approval and to higher education institutions for coursework prescription. Education contracts are complicated by the amount of other materials that are added to the text, such as illustrations, tables, graphs and other learning tools. The situation is further complicated with technology and the use of digital assets, including software that is used to convert simple textbooks into learning materials. This calls for more complex contracts and agreements with different participants. Where applicable and possible, the toolkit will attempt to cite differences in contractual considerations.

We hope these notes will prove useful to inquiring authors, new and developing publishers (or agents) and members of newly-founded writers' or publishers' associations who wish to better understand the general structure and possible terms of publishing agreements so they can manage their professional relationships effectively. We hope that this toolkit may prove a particularly useful reference for those in emerging markets where publishing structures are still in development. In these markets publishers may not have easy access to guidance and resources around issues of authors' rights and copyright legislations, and IP in general. A fair publishing contract is a firm foundation where both the author's and publisher's interests are recognized and obligations clearly addressed.

This toolkit is not, however, a recommendation of a set of specific terms of agreement or legal advice, especially given the many relevant jurisdictions and systems in play, but an attempt to explain key contractual terms and their crucial role in good practice. Similarly, this toolkit is not intended to override or manifest standard contracts negotiated or yet to be negotiated, or common remuneration and other rules between, for example, authors' organizations and publishing trade bodies.

In addition, this toolkit is particularly applicable to the legal framework outside the European Union (EU). In the EU, the combination of individual limitations, exceptions and contractual rights combine to give rise to a patchwork of legal norms that together may have a different impact on the individual contract than can be adequately highlighted here in the general overview.

The rich complexity of the world's publishing ecosystem – from self-publishing to tiny independent publishers to big corporates – involves many kinds of publications, with different genres of works crafted, produced and sold or licensed in multiple formats. Readers are offered works in different print formats, as well as e-books and audio, which can be conveyed via a variety of platforms and distribution mechanisms. These rights and formats are sometimes managed by the author directly, but traditionally via a professional author–publisher relationship.

In Anglo-American traditions and especially with general trade books, the author (of trade books) could be represented by a literary agent to help negotiate, sell and steer the management of the author's creative, contractual and commercial interests, though not all authors will have agents. In many emerging markets there are not yet many (or any) established agents, though an author in one country may have an agent based elsewhere if that agent has global expertise. While there may be resistance from publishers towards agents in some territories, gradually more publishing networks are adapting to authors who have agent representation. At the same time, many authors around the world also continue to work directly with publishers, whether by choice or necessity.

The business of "the book" can seem bewildering in its scope once you start to delve more deeply into its many working parts. But at base it is very simple: an author, a text, a publisher, a reader and – binding these parts together – the principle of authors' rights or copyright legislations. The contract is where creative and commercial considerations meet, with the essential safeguards that written agreements provide to both parties. A contract between an author and a publisher (with or without an agent) reflects each party's responsibilities and rights, the potential rewards and how they are shared within that authors' rights or copyright framework.

It is the job of the contract to crystallize the principles governing the central rights and commercial agreement between author and publisher, as clearly and simply yet as accurately as possible. While there are differences in the detail of the contractual approach taken in the publishing cultures of different countries – also influenced by variance in legal systems – in many parts of the world the principles of this working relationship around the creation of a book have developed along broadly similar lines over centuries. Even given profound changes caused by the growth of digital reading and publishing, plus new models including subscription and shared revenue-streaming, the central publishing contract tenets remain vital aspects of the professional publishing relationship. If anything, this is even more crucial in an era of heightened digital piracy and the arrival of artificial intelligence (AI). There are also many challenges to the principles of authors' rights and copyright, and to authors' rights and the publishers' aim to earn fair reward for their individual investment in the making and sharing of quality IP.

At government and regional level there are moves to act against copyrighted material being used to train Large Language Models (LLMs). Currently many publishers', writers' and agents' organizations around the world are seeking to protect human authorship and its value through formulating contractual language, applying to both publisher and author responsibilities, which is appropriate to new scenarios introduced by the widespread release and use of AI tools. It is encouraging that there is an understanding among many organizations, including authors' and publishers' associations, RROs and world bodies like WIPO and UNESCO that AI has its pros and cons. On the one hand it could revolutionize the way content is created and disseminated, and on the other it has significant implications for IP and copyright. It is our hope that the ongoing deliberations will result in a viable balance.

2 What is publishing?

2.1 The value chain in summary

Let us take a step back to consider the nature and scope of the enterprise of publishing itself. The value chain starts with the author and the work, without which there cannot be a publication. Publishing is about making IP available or fashioning original works into forms accessible to the public, in a way that remunerates the author and those who contribute to the development of the work into published formats. Authors work with publishers so that they can access a range of expertise, to fine-tune the work and make it more widely available to readers.

In principle, every author has the right to appropriate and proportional remuneration when their work is exploited. At the same time, it is up to each author to decide how to deal with their work and, for example, if they wish, to make parts of it available without remuneration systems. Retailers and publishers are part of the value chain and a proper contract with the publisher producing the work makes all the crucial parameters clear. These range from author delivery and production timings to what the author receives per copy for various formats and sale or other licensing arrangements, and what the further duties of the publishing house are. The agreed wording will also stipulate for how long the contract will remain valid, under what conditions, what happens if there are disputes, and when the contract is terminated, bearing in mind that in some countries, this is governed by law.

While most contractual principles have been in place for many decades, since the 1990s global publishing has seen dramatic development. There has been swift technological acceleration as digital delivery models have developed, along with online bookselling, and some elements of publishing contracts have evolved accordingly. For example, clauses have been introduced about licensing additional formats, such as audio, and thus the need for new considerations, such as narrator approval by, or consultation with, the author. Currently there are many debates around audio and e-book subscription and streaming, open access (OA), AI and other questions sparked by technological possibilities. But again, in fair contracts, clear core principles endure and publishers and authors must seek to find common contractual ground and adapt to such developments in a way that protects copyright, mutual interest and human creative endeavour.

2.1.1 The roles of the main parties

At the heart of it lies the work: a writer (or translator) and their text, an illustrator (or photographer) and their images. Around the work are mutual commitments between the author and publisher. The author has written, or commits to write, a book, which the author will complete and edit (in collaboration with the editing department of the publisher) within a certain time frame. The publisher commits to edit and publish the work to a certain standard, within a certain length of time from signature of contract, or from acceptable final delivery of the text if writing or editing is still in progress.

Usually, in principle, the author grants the publisher the exclusive right to exploit the work for their mutual benefit for the duration of their agreement, whether a number of years or the full term of authors' rights or copyright legislations. Publishers are book trade professionals who can enhance the quality and packaging of the author's work through editing and design, and invest through their marketing, sales, distribution and revenue-collecting efforts.

Publishers manage the work throughout its published life, all the way through the value chain (see Section 2.3). The chain begins either with a work commissioned by a publisher, or with a manuscript which has been submitted by an author (or an agent on the author's behalf). The work continues through the editorial and production process, then via marketing and distribution and further in issuing new editions and reprints. In this process the publisher ensures that the work is consistently available, including reprinting current editions and producing new editions (with corrected or additional content or redesigned jackets) where necessary. This continues until the demand for the work is exhausted, or the publisher is unable to meet market need, at which point the rights should revert to the author (see Section 4.19).

2.1.2 Licensing

The contract sets out the agreed language and territory in which the publisher is licensed to publish the work. It also grants the publisher the right to print, copy and distribute the work in various formats - that is, the primary or "volume" rights (for instance, hardback and paperback formats, and often also the e-book formats). In order to maximize the benefit for both author and publisher, in certain instances the publisher may license third parties to exploit the work further, according to their specific areas of expertise. These secondary or subsidiary rights may include:

- translations into other languages;
- publishing in the same language in other regions;
- producing in other formats such as large print or audio; or
- specialized adaptation for other reader groups, as with educational editions or graphic novels.

In some countries, the contract will also include provisions regarding the collective management of the work, via corresponding collective management organizations (CMOs), which often manage secondary rights such as copying in copy shops, lending in public libraries or the legal transfer of files via USB sticks.

The publisher might also sell licenses for serialization, the publishing of extracts in magazines or newspapers (serial rights) or the right for the work to be read on radio. Less often, in general trade publishing, a publisher might control the rights to sell on film, television, theater adaptations (screen and dramatic rights) and products linked to characters in the book (merchandizing). However, in many cases these may be retained by the author, to handle themselves or to work with agents or other specialists directly. The relationship between the author and the publisher and what aspects of the work's life is shared between them is governed by a contractual agreement, which spells out the parties' rights and duties. Publishers tend to want to retain as many of the rights as possible and authors should think carefully about which rights to grant to the publisher. The author should consider the options available to them and the capacity and ability of the publisher to exploit those rights, especially as authors often tend to be in a weaker position when they grant a license or transfer their rights.

2.1.3 Self-publishing

Some authors are currently taking advantage of rapidly developing digital and print technologies and social media platforms to publish and promote their own work. Many who are technically skilled see the benefits of self-publishing in terms of their retention of the full income from the digital, print-on-demand (POD) or short-run printing sales. Still, most authors prefer to collaborate with publishers with professional editing, copy-editing, proofreading, design and distribution channels via retail book chains (and supermarkets in some markets), and to maximize the work's impact by reaching more retailers and readers through a publisher's established infrastructure and contacts. Self-publishing, without a third-party publisher, calls for different measures in terms of printing and sales arrangements, not discussed here.

2.1.4 Support for authors

In some instances, depending on the traditional arrangements and market circumstances, authors will choose to work through an agent, if they can secure one, to generally manage their literary affairs. The agent may help to shape and edit the work before submitting it to publishers, negotiating the terms of the author's deal and contract with publishers and also selling certain rights directly on the author's behalf. These rights, which the author may wish to retain and not grant to the publisher, may include, for example, some territorial, translation and film, television and theater and other adaptation rights. Both author and publisher need to have a good understanding of their options so that they can enter into agreements that benefit both optimally, as far as possible. In brokering deals and negotiating contracts, literary agents act for the author and are paid by the author via a commission percentage of all the author's earnings for the life of those contracts.

Authors can also work directly with local writer development organizations or national authors' associations (where these exist) to get advice on crucial issues. Publishers and (currently to a lesser extent) agents in different countries have trade associations which can address relevant issues, though care should be taken to make sure that such advice and collaboration does not violate national competition laws. In some cases, standard agreements referencing good practice have been developed between authors' associations and publishers' associations and these are useful for both authors and publishers to refer to. But, equally, any author can acquire the necessary tools to understand and negotiate contracts. Authors' associations in particular play an important role in this. These can, for example, give their members model contracts or free recommendations (provided the national competition regulations allow them to do so). Authors' organizations can also conclude binding standard contracts with publishing associations in some jurisdictions.

Publishers need to make sure that they can exploit the rights that they acquire effectively, and authors need to deliver work of a good standard, according to what has been agreed. Both parties should communicate clearly and be supportive of each other in the writing, editing and publishing process, with a clear understanding of their responsibilities when it comes to the publisher's marketing strategy and the author's involvement in publicity. An open, well-managed relationship between the publisher and the author (with or without an agent) can be a mutually rewarding, and, in some cases, a lifelong one, resulting in multiple publications and earnings for the parties. While the contract is a crucial tool in this process, it is not a substitute for good relationship management. The ideal scenario is for all parties to work transparently for mutual benefit, to communicate clearly and to empower each other to do their work as well as possible.

2.2 Authors, publishers and authors' rights or copyright

Who "owns" a work? The author is the owner of their IP, the work of the mind. Once an author has expressed or laid down their original ideas through writing or recording, the form of expression of those ideas becomes protected by authors' rights legislation or copyright law (the wording differs according to the legislation from country to country). Authors may be advised to keep dated evidence of their original work, such as manuscripts and electronic files, to prove their ownership of the work, including when they sent such work to publishers, agencies or reviewers. There is no copyright simply in ideas, but in the original expression of those ideas, in words or images. The question of what constitutes this "originality" can differ from jurisdiction to jurisdiction.

There is no one unified international copyright law and authors' rights and rights to the work may be protected in different ways in different countries. Legally, authors' rights systems, as in France for example, focus on the author as a person and on the author's moral rights, and copyright focuses on the work itself, with copyright as a form of use of the work. In the practical management of remuneration for works there is much overlap, as in both systems the person who made the work, the author, is in control of the work's use.

2.2.1 The history of copyright law

Copyright law and authors' rights have developed around the world over centuries. In 1710 the first copyright statute, the Statute of Anne, was proclaimed in England as "An act for the encouragement of learning, by vesting the copies of printed books in the authors or purchasers of such copies, during the times therein mentioned." Gradually its provisions were widened from the copying of books only, to include a variety of creative works including translations. In France, it was in 1792 that the first IP protection was given to writers of plays, to protect them from state censorship, for example, or from piracy and plagiarism. Different countries' copyright or authors' rights systems have been revised through international and regional agreements. One example is the (Revised) Berne Convention for the Protection of Literary and Artistic Works, which was first established in 1886, and then went through various iterations after negotiations in 1896 (Paris), 1908 (Berlin), 1928 (Rome), 1948 (Brussels), 1967 (Stockholm) and 1971 (Paris).[1]

2.2.2 The scope of copyright

Authors' rights or copyright come into effect when the work is created, in writing or otherwise. Thus authors may hold authors' rights or copyright in works as diverse as the content of letters and the texts of speeches and interviews as well as books, poems, short stories, essays and songs, where these exist in some form of written notation, or electronically retrievable format, including audio. "Literary works" are legally defined as works that are written, spoken or sung - also including tables and compilations, databases, computer programs and their preparatory design material. It is worth remembering the distinction that this is about the *expression* of the content not the physical object - so the recipient of a letter owns the physical manifestation of those words but cannot publish it without the letter-writer's permission. (Note that in some jurisdictions, especially where there is a fair use provision like in the United States of America, this permission may not be required.) Similarly, an author owns their own paper manuscript and can sell that on to a collector, but the collector may not publish the contents if the author does not allow it or has already granted rights exclusively to a publisher.

What does copyright mean to an owner (in the case of heirs or assigns - that is, those to whom a right or liability is legally transferred, in cases where the underlying legislation permits such a transfer)? They are able to authorize or prevent:

- reproduction (copying);
- distribution of those copies;
- communication to the public in terms of performances, broadcasts, displays and interactive programs;
- rental and loan of the work;
- the making of translations and adaptations of the work; and
- the work being made available online.

Furthermore, the integrity of the author's work plays a major role, which means that the author can, for example, refuse to have their book abridged or changed. This is relevant in the editing process, for example, or in the creation of abridged audiobooks or Reader's Digest editions.

The IP (text or illustrations) that the author submits to the publisher belongs to the author, while the copyright in the design and production materials of the published book belongs to the publisher. The author licenses the copyright to the publisher to exploit and protect the work for mutual benefit. This arrangement remains in place for (a) a restricted time (8, 12 or 20 years, for example), or (b) for the length of copyright (usually 50 to 70 years after the author's death, depending on national law). After the author's death it is transferred to the author's literary estate, heirs or assigns, for as long as the publisher continues to exploit the work, until the expiry of the contract or the length of copyright.

1 You can read more about the detail of the Convention on the WIPO website, along with further information on the subsequent WIPO Copyright Treaty (1996) and background to copyright treaties: www.wipo.int/treaties/en/ip/berne/summary_berne.html; www.wipo.int/treaties/en/ip/wct/; www.wipo.int/treaties/

Although authors' rights and copyright in the work belong to the author, if they have licensed a set of exclusive rights to the publisher they cannot then use that work in a manner that competes with the publication during the term of license. However, use for promotional purposes, such as short extracts on the author's own website, may be mutually beneficial and reasonably agreed. Unless the rights are non-exclusively granted, authors must get the publisher's written permission to use material independently, including for use in other publications, unless for reserved rights that have remained outside of the licensing agreement.

2.2.3 Reversion of copyright

The license may revert to the author regardless of the length of the contract if the work is out of print or no longer on the market due to there being no demand or decreased demand for the work. It may also revert for other reasons such as if the publisher decides not to continue, goes bankrupt or winds up the company. Such eventualities and assurance of reversion of the license are covered in specific reversion and liquidation clauses in contracts or in some national legislations. These are vital to safeguard authors' rights and economic opportunities when a publisher has ceased to successfully deploy the copyright or has been forced to cease trading. Note that in some countries reversion of rights is governed by law, or different approaches may be taken to print and electronic editions. Parties to the contract should comply with such national laws and standards, where applicable.

2.2.4 Visual creators

Publishers will often bring together the copyright work of the writers along with creators of visual material, whose work is held under separate copyright. A vast array of added IP for books is created by:

- illustrators of children's books and graphic novels;
- compilers of tables, maps and charts in educational books;
- designers of illustrative motifs for novels; and
- photographers whose work might be the subject of a whole art book, or whose photographs are used for how-to manuals, cookbooks, memoirs, biographies and cover designs.

Where a publisher develops the concept of a book and orchestrates the contributions of different parties (for instance, in a short story or poetry anthology) there might be an arrangement where each contributor retains copyright in their work and grants a license for its use to the publisher in this context, receiving an agreed share and ongoing royalty portion. Alternatively, depending on the jurisdiction, especially in countries influenced by the US legal tradition, the publisher might devise and develop a project where they own the copyright in the overall project, with contributors agreeing to complete their input as "work for hire" for a set fee and no ongoing income share. Work produced by an employee of a publishing house in the course of their work on a book would, in countries inspired by US-style systems, belong to the publisher and would not be copyright of the individual. This is not the case in countries that have authors' rights systems where there are separate contracts for employment and the license of their IP.

2.2.5 Reproduction and piracy

It is of course vital to consider the rights of the original writers and copyright holders when wishing to quote from and reproduce literary and graphic works to an extent that exceeds what is permitted under applicable copyright law. Publishers and authors need to be clear on whether they have the right to use the work if they wish to:

- compile anthologies of essays, stories or poems;
- quote sections of copyright work;
- reproduce diagrams, graphs, tables or an artist's images in a book, or accompanying an article or blog.

Written permission should always be sought where works are in copyright and uncertainty on this score is no excuse for not securing appropriate permissions. It is important here to acquaint yourself with the distinctions in national copyright laws, for instance, between countries inspired by "fair dealing" in the United Kingdom and "fair use" in the United States. There are numerous other jurisdictional variations, based on a system of clearly outlined exceptions and limitations, such as in the EU.

Publishers help protect their authors' works by ensuring that there is no unauthorized use or piracy. Where illegal copying or even illegal sale happens, they must take the necessary action to ensure that the illegal use is stopped and, where possible, pursue options for both parties to receive compensation for the unlawful use of the material. Such enforcement activities often require significant resources, which the author usually does not have.

For more detailed resources on copyright and piracy and copyright theft questions see Useful links. Some specific resources are also given below:

- A basic copyright summary is provided by the Authors' Licensing and Collecting Society (ALCS).[2]
- For more detailed resources on authors' rights legislation and other rules of the European sector, contact can be made with the European Writers' Council (EWC)[3] or the European Council of Literary Translators' Associations (CEATL).[4]
- Publishers may contact the Federation of European Publishers (FEP).[5]

It is worth noting here that recent swift developments in generative AI have focused attention more sharply on many major LLMs using vast amounts of unlicensed copyright material for machine learning training, with the European AI Act proposals responding to this [6] and the UK's Publishers Association putting out a statement that their members do not authorize the use of their copyright-protected works in relation to the training, development or operation of AI models, outside of any agreed licensing arrangements.[7] There is a widespread insistence that generative AI models can and should be developed in a legal and sustainable manner. Similar statements have been made and embraced by publishers' and authors' organizations in other territories, making it clear that while publishers may use AI in their operational work, AI models must be developed in a legal, sustainable and ethical manner. A copyright licensing is aan appropriate approach to ensure consent and remuneration for copyright-protected works being used to develop generative AI models. As a result some new entrants to the LLM field are starting to seek licenses for 'fair training', as welcomed by the US Authors Guild.[8]

2.2.6 Assignment of copyright

In some countries with copyright laws (not authors' rights legislation), authors may *license* to publishers the right to use their IP (under varying arrangements according to circumstances). They generally should not *assign* their copyright, which means they would transfer ownership of the copyright completely and are no longer the copyright owner in that work. When rights are assigned to a publisher, an author effectively loses control of the editing of their text and relinquishes the right to credit for reproduction of the work. With assignment, even if the publisher goes bankrupt the copyright does not automatically revert to the author. Assignment of authors' copyright is not standard practice in trade publishing, as it is not necessary for successful publishing and damages authors' incomes and long-term prospects. While authors are asked to assign copyright more routinely in academic and university press contracts, an exclusive license is sufficient, as copyright assignment is not needed to license subsidiary rights or protect copyright. A straightforward request to substitute a license for assignment wording will often be successful and ensure the author has not signed all rights away and is therefore able to use their own work in future publications as long as there is no conflict with an exclusive license.[9] Exceptions to this general rule might be projects produced by the publisher with teams of authors, such as encyclopedias, and some textbooks, reference works and compilations.

2 www.alcs.co.uk/copyright-basics-for-writers
3 https://europeanwriterscouncil.eu
4 www.ceatl.eu
5 https://fep-fee.eu
6 https://www.europarl.europa.eu/topics/en/article/20230601STO93804/eu-ai-act-first-regulation-on-artificial-intelligence
7 https://www2.societyofauthors.org/2024/03/11/publishers-withhold-use-of-copyright-protected-works-to-develop-large-language-models-in-letter-to-ai-companies/
8 https://authorsguild.org/news/ag-supports-fairly-trained-ai-licensing-model/
9 An example from the Authors Guild (AG) of America can be found here: www.authorsguild.org/industry-advocacy/authors-keep-your-copyrights-you-earned-them/

Authors who, depending on the jurisdiction, can and do assign their copyright, may still be eligible for Public Lending Right (PLR) in relevant territories and also receive payments from collective management organizations, depending on the legal context in the relevant country.

In any publishing practice it is important to bear in mind that there is no one unified international copyright law, and that different copyright and authors' rights systems may pertain depending on where you are publishing or being published.

2.3 The publishing value chain and process

2.3.1 The origin of a published work

The publishing value chain usually starts with the author's work, that is, the conception and writing. However, this may vary in areas such as educational publishing to include the following stages:

- market or education needs researched by the publisher;
- identification of the appropriate author;
- workshops and training around the requirements; and
- writing and development of the manuscript, often with more than one contributor, including text, graphs, tables or illustrations.

Often, in trade publishing, especially fiction, the author writes a book and either seeks a publisher directly or, in some instances, approaches them through an agent. Today more and more authors, especially in larger (or more electronically enabled) markets, are opting to self-publish and promote their own books through distributors or direct to retailers both in print and e-book formats. Good publishers add value through their work in areas such as editorial and design input, financing the development of the book, warehousing and distribution, copyright protection, and exploitation of secondary rights. Agents can also add value through negotiating better deals for authors with publishers, selling secondary rights and protecting the rights of their authors. Some authors choose to focus on their writing and depend on their publisher or agent for the rest of the business, though with final say on contractual or financial decisions, while others prefer to do everything themselves including managing their rights. There are pros and cons to either approach and authors must think carefully about their means, know-how and capacity before deciding on an approach.

The value chain of educational publishing often differs from trade publishing, but there can be overlap. In some publications such as biography and other non-fiction publications, the publisher can come up with an idea and commission an author to write a particular book, in the same way that an educational publisher would commission an author. Similarly, some education authors, especially of general education materials, proactively generate ideas and write books and then approach appropriate publishers to consider their work for publishing.

Figure 1 shows a simple workflow for a publisher-commissioned project . At the point of a finished book, other formats such as e-book will come into play at the same time as printing.

Figure 1: A simple workflow for a publisher-commissioned project
Source: Brian Wafawarowa.

Figure 1 is more elaborate for education publishing, where the value chain is more complex. As indicated earlier regarding education publishing, the publisher commissions suitable authors to write and develop learning materials along the specific needs of the national curriculum. The publisher and the author work together to workshop the materials with learners and teachers to ensure their effectiveness as learning tools. The publisher and the author prepare the materials for approval by education authorities. This can include complex learning tools such as digital assets, assessments and feedback mechanisms. The publisher and the author continue to work together throughout the life cycle of the education material to make sure that it remains relevant to the learning needs and that teachers and learners are adequately trained about using the materials.

2.3.2 Added value by the publisher

Generally speaking, after the author has written the manuscript, the publisher adds further value to the manuscript in the following ways:

- peer review (in the case of academic publishing);
- content editing;
- copy-editing and proofreading;
- commissioning and developing illustrations and other graphic material; and
- designing the book, including the cover.

2.3.3 Payment

Note that, as explained above, with trade publishing, especially fiction, the process most often starts with the author writing the work and approaching the publisher or agent. The publisher is also responsible for financing the whole process, including, in some cases for both trade and education publishing, an advance payment to the author. Advance payments are more common practice in trade publishing because the writing work is done by the author prior to engaging a publisher, which is not as often the case in education publishing.

2.3.4 Translation

If a publisher wants to publish the work of an author who writes in another language, they may acquire the rights after reading a sample translated by a competent (human) translator and will commission a full translation and work with a translator to edit the final text. In some cases, the author or original-language publisher might offer a complete translation in order to facilitate a sale. Depending on the agreement, some publishers pay translators a lump sum for their work, without royalties, while some publishers pay the translator an advance and royalties. Often the translator royalty is achieved by reducing the authors' royalty and allocating that percentage to the translator. Authors and translators (with or without agents) will need to clarify and negotiate with publishers accordingly.

2.3.5 Illustrations and photography

With children's and other illustrated and art books the publisher also works with visual artists, photographers and designers. Illustrators and photographers should also earn co-contributor royalties for significant co-creation input, though this can vary according to contractual work-for-hire arrangements when the illustrative material is a less significant part of the whole.

2.3.6 Re-editioning, distribution and sales

In the field of education and some non-fiction publishing, the publisher ensures that the book remains up to date and relevant by working with the author to develop new editions linked to changing curriculum or examination requirements. In all cases, the publisher also ensures that the book is available consistently, through reprinting, stocking and distributing the book, in print and digital formats (often using intermediary distributors and wholesalers) to ensure the book reaches retailers, libraries and educational institutions, who are the direct window to readers. The publisher is responsible for promoting the work to users, from general readers seeking entertainment or information in trade publishing, to learners and teachers in the case of educational books. Some publishers - in particular smaller independent publishers or those covering specialist areas such as poetry, art, academic journals or niche subject matter - may sell a large proportion of their authors' work directly to readers via their websites. They may drive traffic for sales using social media platforms, newsletters, writer events and festivals.

2.4 The author's responsibilities

The author is responsible for writing their own original work and making sure that the manuscript is delivered to the publisher on time and as per agreement. Failure to deliver the (final) manuscript may have significant consequences for the author, including the need to pay back an advance. The work should not contravene the law in any way - for instance, it should not be libelous or involve any plagiarism. The copyright of other authors must be respected and any relevant permissions need to be cleared; the writer (or in some cases, the publisher) must seek and gain written permission to reproduce photographs or illustrations and other writers' copyright work. Likewise, the author must ensure that they do not violate any personal rights of third parties.

You can read more on the author's warranties in Section 4.4 below. For further information about basic guidance on copyrights and permissions, contact national authors' or publishers' associations, where they exist.[10]

Beyond the contract and in certain works, including works of fiction, memoirs and biographical works, it may be advisable to have a disclaimer at the beginning of the book. A disclaimer asserts, for example in the case of a novel, that the book is a work of fiction and any resemblance of characters to known, living or dead people is purely coincidental. In a work of historical fiction, the disclaimer may state that certain historical events are true, but that characters and situations are imagined. A memoir writer might include a disclaimer to say that names have been changed and some characters are composites of several people in order to make them unidentifiable. The intention of such disclaimers is to reduce the risk of lawsuits and unfavorable outcomes in the event of a lawsuit.

After delivery, the author must consider editorial feedback and make corrections and revisions as requested by the publisher. The author is not obliged to accept these changes, due to the right of integrity of their work; disagreements may arise and need to be resolved as amicably and mutually as possible. Both parties need to cooperate to make sure that they produce a book

10 The UK Society of Authors offers basic guidance on copyrights and permissions here: https://www2.societyofauthors.org/advice/guides/

of the best quality possible. In the case of non-fiction, the author may need to revise the work for subsequent editions (if agreed in the contract) to ensure that the work remains relevant and up to date, especially in the case of educational and special interest books.

2.4.1 Joint authorship

Some publications have more than one author; this is especially common in the case of textbooks. In some cases the authors' contributions are separately identifiable, for instance through chapters or other sections of the book. In other cases their contributions cannot be separated and are not intended to be distinguishable. Sometimes disputes can arise between co-authors, and working relationships may break down, which can negatively impact on the publication of the work. The publisher, having invested in the development of the work, may not be able to exploit the disputed work further, for example with updates and subsequent editions. It is thus preferable, where possible, to distinguish the individual authors' contributions.

It is crucial for co-authors originating content to have a clear agreement between themselves, which should include details regarding payment, credit and division of work, as well as provisions for the end of the creative relationship. Also, they must decide if they want one contract each with the publisher or one combined contract. If there is a separate contract each, the terms should be transparent to all parties. Where publishers commission multiple authors to work on a project, the publishers and the authors should also agree on what happens in the event of a dispute, including the following:

- continuation of the work between the authors who want to continue;
- the right of the remaining authors to continue with the work and subsequent editions;
- separation agreements and compensation for the authors who cannot continue;
- the inclusion of additional authors; and
- provision for mediation between the authors.

Publishers and authors must ensure that there are proper agreements that allow them to proceed with the remaining authors or recruit new authors in the event of one or some of the authors dying or not being in a position to continue, while preserving the departing or deceased authors' rights.

2.5 The publisher's responsibilities

The publisher is responsible for the development and improvement of the manuscript, financing the publishing process, warehousing and distribution, marketing, promoting and selling the work, ensuring that the work remains available and relevant and protecting the work from unauthorized use and other violations. This includes acting against offenders and financing such action. In situations where there is unauthorized use of the work or any copyright infringement, the publisher usually finances legal and remedial action and indemnifies the author from any harm that may arise from the process.

2.5.1 Author names

It is the publisher's role to ensure that titles and the names of authors (and illustrators and translators) are appropriately visible on every edition and listed on catalogs and data feeds, along with the correct metadata and keywords, and to keep these listings up to date. Authors' names should always be on the front cover, unless it is educational content, or sometimes non-fiction, when there are several authors. Practices in different markets around translator names on the front cover vary, though there is a strong international campaign for the names of translators (and illustrators) to also appear on front covers.

2.5.2 Payment

The publisher has an obligation to pay an agreed percentage of the revenue generated from the work to the author as a royalty fee. The royalty is paid periodically as stipulated in the contract, twice-yearly or annually. Failure to pay royalties accordingly is a serious breach. As the author has already invested in the work to be published through expertise, research, development of the idea into an outline and in some cases fully completing the manuscript, it is good practice for the publisher to pay an up-front sum, usually called an advance payment, to be set against the sums acquired through future sales. This sum is to be seen as a guaranteed and non-refundable amount, regardless of whether the sales succeed in recouping this advance or not. The guaranteed sum will also be retained by the author if the publisher either does not publish in the time specified in the contract despite manuscript acceptance, or decides not to produce the book for other reasons.

In situations where, by agreement, the author is responsible for activities and inputs such as indexes and illustrations, the publisher pays for such activities and may deduct the fees or part of the fees from the author's future earnings, as agreed between the author and the publisher in the contract. With photographs and illustrations for non-fiction books in the general trade, the publisher may fund the permission costs for the illustrative material up to a certain cap, after which the author may pay for any excess via deduction from earnings. With non-fiction in particular, it is important to determine during the initial negotiation the detail of who will pay for (and do) what in terms of text, image permissions and indexing, so that there is no need for wrangling, confusion and potential bad feeling later.

2.5.3 Relevance and demand

In consultation with the author, the publisher is also responsible for continuous assessment of the relevance of the work and may decide that the demand for the work has ceased. As detailed above, where the publisher ceases printing and the work is not available on the market, or sales have significantly slowed, the copyright license should revert to the author. Contracts should be clear on the parameters and process for this, including on publishing an e-book edition of the book. Here, clauses are often developed which say, for example, that if an e-book sells below a certain number of copies within a certain period of time, these rights will also revert to the author (at the latest, at the same time as the print rights revert).

2.5.4 Design

The physical design of the work as manifested in production files usually belongs to the publisher, who will have paid the designer a salary or fee, but the author retains copyright in their IP and has the right to license the work elsewhere after the termination of a particular commercial relationship, though a new publisher would have to re-set the text or pay the original publisher to use the previous files.

2.6 Traditional publishing models

The international book and publishing sector is vast and comprises many subsectors, offering authors various means of delivering their work to their readers in different formats. The advent of digital publishing has given authors more options for direct customer access, sales and self-promotion. Publishers have also become more versatile in terms of their publishing options and how they reach readers or listeners. As with many categorizations across the rich and varied field of publishing, there can sometimes be overlap between the descriptions given below.

2.6.1 General, consumer or trade publishing

Depending on the jargon used in different regions, general, consumer or trade publishing refers to non-educational or non-professional publishing of general content that is meant for the wide direct market or general population. It is a very broad sector that includes fiction of all kinds and for all ages, poetry, memoir, biography, self-help books and other texts that are sold directly to the public via online and bricks-and-mortar retailers. These are the books readers will see reviewed in newspapers, on bestseller lists and adapted for other formats like audio, radio, and film and television, including both fiction and non-fiction and popular reference works.

2.6.2 Educational and academic publishing

Educational publishing forms the backbone of the publishing sector in many economically developing countries. For example, across Africa, educational publishing constitutes as much as 95 percent of all publishing output.[11] Educational publishing may thus help to subsidize the limited amount of trade and other publishing activity in certain regions.

Publishing for formal educational purposes can cover school textbooks, study guides and general materials, as well as college, university and other tertiary education texts, in both text and digital formats. Textbooks that are written to the requirements of the curriculum and usually to specific requirements for selection by state or federal education authorities form educational publishing's mainstay. Although the school textbook market can be lucrative, it requires heavy up-front investment and is vulnerable to adverse policy changes and under-investment by the state.

Academic and scientific publishing is mainly concerned with the production and distribution of works of scholarly research through journals, non-fiction books and online resources. There are fast-moving and complex developments and debates in academic publishing around OA and open educational resources (OERs). OA refers to materials that are freely available for anyone to use in their existing form; they may not be revised, repurposed or redistributed without the permission of the rights holder. OER refers to teaching, learning or research materials that are in the public domain where users are allowed to use as is, repurpose or tailor the materials according to their teaching or learning needs. The material can be shared or altered without permission or attribution.

There is a significant difference in the range of rights granted in educational, academic and scholarly publishing contracts and those granted in trade publishing, and also different expectations regarding returns, so royalty levels and terms may vary accordingly.

2.6.3 Professional and specialist publishing

Professional and specialist publishing is concerned with narrow and highly specialized niche subjects or content. Professional publishing output might include manuals for certain trades, or handbooks for professions, such as those dealing with issues specific to lawyers, doctors or accountants. Specialist publishing might cover publications of specific interest, such as books on regional birds or insects, or arts and crafts such as embroidery or tattoos. Due to limited reader numbers and the specialized skills and knowledge that are required for this niche publishing, professional and specialist publishing tends to have limited economies of scale and the books tend to be highly priced, although can be very lucrative for the publisher.

2.7 Alternative publishing models

2.7.1 E-book and digital-first publishing

The development of user-friendly electronic reading devices and the growth of online retail platforms have sharpened readers' appetite for e-books, which often retail at lower prices than print books and can be delivered instantly. Digital publishing is now integral to the publishing process in more and more countries as publishers produce electronic publications alongside, ahead of or sometimes even entirely in place of print.

Demand for e-books is particularly high in certain genres such as true crime and self-help in non-fiction, and crime, mystery, romance, science fiction and fantasy in fiction. It is in these areas that we see the greatest flourishing of digital-first publishing (where the book appears first in digital format, as opposed to simultaneous with the print edition), or even digital-only publishing (where a book is not printed at all but is only made available in digital format). Most digital-first publishers will, however, also seek to capitalize on a successful title by providing print editions via POD technology, if they have licensed the rights to do so.

The availability of digital technology in schools and other educational institutions, together with teacher readiness, has promoted the uptake of digital content in educational publishing, further accelerated by the COVID-19 pandemic and the necessity of online teaching during lockdowns.

11 As cited in the African Publishers' Network (APNET)/Association for the Development of Education in Africa (ADAE) Survey, 2000.

Many trade publishers granted free use of content during these lockdowns, but there is a need for a return to licensing models to ensure a balance of learner access and author remuneration.

However, a stark digital divide still exists between dominant and emerging publishing markets. Despite high-profile initiatives such as One Laptop Per Child, in some parts of the developing world and some parts of the developed world, digital publishing in education and leisure reading has not gained as much ground as might have been expected. This is due to lack of infrastructure and hardware, poor bandwidth, electricity and wi-fi provision limitations, and data costs.

Good quality yet affordable e-book publishing is an important aspect in the battle against digital piracy, in order to provide visible, reliable alternatives to illegal "free" reading, which is damaging to creative sectors around the world.

2.7.2 Self-publishing, vanity publishing and hybrid publishing

Digital technology has significantly reduced the cost of self-publishing and distribution and facilitated options for direct author-to-reader access. E-book self-publishing has enabled authors with the necessary organizational and promotional skills to sell their own books without the need to invest in producing quantities of print copies, with accompanying warehousing costs. Online platforms have provided authors with the possibility of testing their work with readers through blogging, podcasts and online reader feedback. Digital technology has enabled many authors to promote their own work through digital marketing and promotions, including on social networks. Some independent authors are eventually published by traditional publishers after launching successful self-publishing careers.

Beyond completely independent self-publishing, there are hybrid models where companies offer publishing services to aspiring authors (also known as hybrid, partnership, custom, contribution, contributory or subsidy publishing). There are also exploitative vanity publishing outfits, where authors end up paying the publisher both for production services and the marketing of the book and are often charged high prices for very limited numbers of copies of their own published material and poor or non-existent promotion of the work. Authors need to be careful when considering these options, where discerning exactly what is on offer can be confusing and, especially in the case of disreputable vanity publishing, couched in extremely alluring language.

Authors who are uncertain of publishers' reputations should scrutinize their websites carefully and check whether they are members of their country's national publishing associations. Checking with local booksellers as to whether the publishers' books are stocked can also be helpful, as can seeking the advice of local writer development agencies and writers' unions where possible.[12]

2.8 The role of the literary agent

Literary agents act on behalf of authors: they identify promising authors, help them develop their work and generally look after their business interests. This includes finding appropriate publishers, who may even compete for a promising title, and negotiating the best deal possible with the acquiring publisher. Good agents have networks of publishing or sub-agent contacts around the world and can promote their authors' titles to many appropriate publishers, using their websites and rights catalogs, direct meetings and book fairs. They maximize the earning potential of their clients' work by directly selling further rights such as film, television and theater, and translations into foreign languages, especially in larger markets such the Anglo-America jurisdictions or Germany, the People's Republic of China and South America.

Agents help steer the author's career, provide financial oversight of an author's income and help ensure that the author is correctly and promptly paid. Good agents not only represent their clients on rights sales and contracts: they also liaise between author and publisher on

12 See, for example: https://societyofauthors.org/News/News/2022/April/Writers-unions-call-for-reform-of-the-%E2%80%98hybrid%E2%80%99

other matters, including questions around titles and covers and ensuring that the publisher promotes and sells their client's work effectively. By dealing with strategic, contractual and commercial matters for their clients, literary agents free up time for their authors, so they can devote their energies to writing. Agents always receive a contractually fixed percentage share of each fee paid to the author (the agent's commission). Authors should be cautious of any agent who asks for a lump sum or reading fee to be paid in advance, going against the established commission approach.

2.9 From books to other formats

Beyond the primary publishing rights and the selling of physical and digital copies of books, authors can increase the income on their creative work through the strategic exploitation of further format and adaptation rights, such as audio, radio, film and television, and translation.

While some publishers want to acquire and sell on as wide a range of rights as possible, taking a percentage of the royalties and passing the share on to the author, authors may wish to retain a selection of key subsidiary rights, for themselves or an agent to sell. In cases where authors license these subsidiary rights to the publisher as part of the overall deal, the publisher either promotes and sells those rights themselves via their in-house rights and contracts teams or finds an independent agent who can do so on their behalf. Literary agents can play an important role in seeking wider revenue opportunities directly for their authors or for a publisher, if an agent is acting for a publisher as client. Note that an agent would never act for both publisher and author in a deal.

The negotiation regarding the extent of various potential rights to be granted depends on the situation, including availability of agents, the nature of the author's work, the negotiating possibilities (including whether publishers are in a competitive situation bidding for the work) and the author's existing relationship with the publisher. It is important for the author to ensure that their publisher can effectively exploit all the rights that they want to secure in their contract. The author must decide whether the publisher has the necessary skill and capacity and a good track record in selling such rights, and monitoring outcomes.

Sublicensed percentage splits as divided between author and publisher can vary greatly according to precedents and specific negotiation situations. It is also important for authors to have approval on adaptations of their work and approval (or consultation) may also be required for certain other sub rights, depending on negotiation and contract.

The best contract is one that treats and remunerates the author fairly and allows the publisher to make the author's work as widely and effectively available as possible, for mutual benefit. This ideal is summed up well by Lynette Owen (an established freelance rights and copyright consultant who worked for UK publishers in the past), in *Clarke's Publishing Agreements* as "to place rights in the hands of those best able to exploit them in the interest, both of the wide availability of the work and also of income to the author and to those who work for the author."[13]

As technologies, sales channels and reader tastes develop, subsidiary rights will continue to evolve. Details of various subsidiary rights are included in Section 4.15.

13 Owen, L. (ed.) 2006. *Clark's Publishing Agreements: A Book of Precedents*. Seventh Edition. Haywards's Heath: Tottel.

3 Contracts: why and how

The relationships, processes and obligations described above are crucial and complex and cannot be left to verbal agreements or assumed goodwill. They must be clearly spelled out in a written contract, otherwise matters easily become confused, resulting in unpleasant situations, acrimony, failed projects or even litigation. A good contract is a record of agreed parameters and timescales for the writing and delivery (of the text by the author and the finished product by the publisher) and remuneration (by the publisher to the author). It is also a map of the book's production process and future sale and life cycle. A contract is a record of details at the time of signature, and forecasts what is to be expected. Its clauses are designed to act as safety mechanisms in case things do not go according to plan. For instance, it covers scenarios such as if the author fails to deliver a manuscript that meets the contractual specifications, or the publisher fails to publish in a timely fashion, or goes bankrupt, or allows the book to go out of print and off the market, thus triggering a reversion of the license. Each potential default scenario requires that a safety net be in place for the parties before they sign on "the dotted line" (as used to happen with paper contracts).

Publishing deals are concluded in optimism, in the hope of strong sales and critical acclaim when the finished book is launched upon the world. However, all parties to a contract must also have a healthy "what if?" skepticism: there is the possibility that the process might veer off course or become stuck, due to failure by either party to deliver what is contracted in terms of content or service, or when a published book's sales start to falter or cease entirely. These safety net clauses may seem distant possibilities in the warm glow of a fresh deal, but are vital when chill reality and commercial disappointment set in.

In an ideal world, publishers and authors have very good relationships that last the author's whole career. Such publisher–author relationships, like author–agent relationships, are maintained by mutual interest and benefit around the author's work. However, these relationships cannot be left to assumed mutual interest and the anticipation of mutual gain. A contract is necessary to govern the publisher's relationship with the author and to ensure that publishers, authors and other role players are clear about and meet their obligations to each other.

The art of negotiation is a separate subject in itself, but good contracts are built on clear negotiation, where both parties are sure they understand the terms used. Ideally both parties should keep an email trail of the discussions leading to agreement, in order to avoid confusion or disagreement later. It is advisable to use the phrase "subject to contract" along the way, to summarize agreement in a deal memo (a skeleton of the more fully worded contract itself) and for each party to have a checklist of the essential terms so as not to omit anything vital.

While contracts are important as legal documents that spell out the obligations of each party to the agreement, they have their limits and may not be able to cover every future eventuality. Enduring author–publisher relationships are based on fairness, mutual respect and working for mutual benefit. The contract will not prevent every disagreement, but a good relationship between the author and the publisher can survive a contract that does not address some specific thorny issue. Deficiencies that are later discovered can be addressed by mutual agreement in addenda.

3.1 The principle of fair contracts and minimum terms agreements

In many parts of the world, publishers' and authors' associations have worked together to establish fair and viable terms of agreement and in many cases have come up with minimum standards that they encourage their respective members to use as guidelines, or which are even legally binding and may not be undermined. Sometimes these documents are not necessarily agreed to between the professional associations representing authors and publishers but are developed by, for example, authors' associations and writer or creator trade unions to guide their own members in what they should be aware of and ask for. Such associations may then invite publishers to comment or endorse these documents and go on to implement the minimum standards as good practice when they sign agreements, though this also will depend on countries' differing legal frameworks. Some organizations may also release documents to members or on their websites, without publisher endorsement. Much may be gleaned about general principles from these recommendations, though some elements will be specific to their own national circumstances and legal jurisdictions. Sometimes these proposals are not agreed to by individual publishers, or by authors who may prefer otherwise.

The use of such best practice, model contract or minimum terms agreements is voluntary and many individual publishers and authors adapt them for their own use. Some of the minimum terms or guidelines might include, for example, what is regarded as a fair royalty rate, guidelines on the duration of agreements between publishers and authors, and how to terminate or renew such agreements. While minimum terms may be established through negotiations between publishers' and authors' associations, the minimum standards must comply with national law, including what can and cannot be agreed under competition law. In less common cases some governments stipulate these minimum standards, where all publishers and authors must familiarize themselves with such legal requirements and ensure that they comply. However, it is more common to have book sectors where authors, agents and publishers are free to negotiate the terms of their contracts in an informed way, rather than having them stipulated to them by the state. Authors' and publishers' associations can assist their members to make informed decisions through training and sharing of best practice, as legally appropriate. Agents also act to serve their own author clients' best interests with regard to negotiating the best possible terms.

By way of example, the UK Society of Authors has a list of contractual requirements for authors which they have formed into the acronym CREATOR,[14] with recommendations as follows:

C - **C**learer contracts, including written contracts which set out the exact scope of the rights granted.
R - fair **R**emuneration. Equitable and unwaivable remuneration for all forms of exploitation, to include bestseller clauses, so if a work does far better than expected the creator shares in its success even if copyright was assigned.
E - an obligation of **E**xploitation for each mode of exploitation. Also known as the "use it or lose it" clause. This is the French model.
A - fair, understandable and proper **A**ccounting terms.
T - **T**erm. Reasonable and limited contract terms and regular reviews to take into account new forms of exploitation.
O - **O**wnership. Authors, including illustrators and translators, should be appropriately credited for all uses of their work and moral rights should be unwaivable.
R - All other clauses to be subject to a general test of **R**easonableness.

Links to other principles and agreements can be found the Useful links section, bearing in mind the sector- and territory-specific nature of most contracts. These are generally not static documents and must be revisited regularly to develop responses to new commercial and

14 Society of Authors' website (2016): https://societyofauthors.org/Where-We-Stand/C-R-E-A-T-O-R-Campaign-for-Fair-Contracts

technological advances affecting publishers and authors. Each individual negotiation will have to be made on the author's and the work's merits in the context of national and copyright law.

3.2 Boilerplate and standard contracts

Boilerplate agreements are template contract formats that are established over time between the relevant author and publisher, or the author's agent and publisher. They are like minimum terms agreements established between organizations, but decided between individual contracting parties, with or without reference to minimum terms agreements. Boilerplate agreements are a practical expression of multiple negotiations and useful in avoiding the need to renegotiate every detail of the wording of every contract on every deal and publication. The parties agree that provisions of earlier contracts will apply, unless they are specifically renegotiated between the author and the publisher or between the publisher and the agent on behalf of their client.

Examples of clauses that may be covered in a boilerplate agreement include:

- subsidiary rights splits;
- royalties paid on certain quantities in different formats and territories;
- time given to the publisher to exploit certain rights before they revert to the author; and
- royalty rates against different discount rates to retailers (where such discount variables pertain).

Despite the existence of a boilerplate agreement, authors, agents and publishers may be able to renegotiate clauses in the contract with new publications, depending on circumstances - for instance, in the exceptional situation where an author has achieved phenomenal success. In such situations, the specifically negotiated clause or the new product takes precedence over the boilerplate agreement provision but may be explicitly noted as "not to be taken as precedent," so as to be seen to apply to this exceptional case.

In some countries, agreement has been reached across the industry on standard contract terms and a generally standardized form of contract is in wide use. However, in some markets such standard contracts may not have been updated for some time in tandem with technological developments. Where an author has had success or there is competition for rights, variation via negotiation may be possible, unless prohibited by national law.

In some jurisdictions there are contractual term limitations that are specified by law. In such jurisdictions, term agreements between publishers and authors outside the legal provisions are illegal. Publishers and authors must make sure that their agreements are in line with the relevant statutory limitations in their territory.

In countries where legislation prescribes fixed book prices, for instance, the discounts mentioned above do not apply. In such jurisdictions publishers should be careful in their engagements with retailers and distributors in order not to break the law.

4 Publishing contracts: the nuts and bolts

The aim of this discussion is neither to give publishers and authors a set contract template nor to recommend specific boilerplate contracts. The aim is to explain the common and crucial clauses in a publisher–author contract, emphasizing why those clauses are important, what they seek to cover and what authors (along with their agents) and publishers should consider and look out for. There will be some similarities in the general order of information between contracts, but publishing agreements will not follow identical clause ordering and wording may vary widely. The golden rule is always to query what is unclear and make sure that you understand what you are agreeing to before signing any contract. Authors should not be afraid to ask questions of acquiring editors, and to request changes. You would be surprised how many people, even seasoned executives, are unclear on the details and implications of contracts they have signed.

4.1 The preamble: parties to the contract and brief scope of work

The preamble is the first part of a publishing agreement, the introduction to the contract. As with a personal introduction, it clearly names and identifies the parties to the agreement. These parties are those who are taking on the legal obligations laid out in the pages that follow, which could include:

- the author;
- the author's estate;
- the author or copyright owner's company name;
- co-authors;
- illustrators;
- translators;
- the agent; and
- the publisher.

The preamble includes the parties and entities that are bound by the agreement, including the publishing imprint or imprints to which the agreement applies or the entities to which the agreement may be assigned, or the successors in the event of the author's death or incapacitation. The author (or copyright owner or proprietor) and the publisher will sign the agreement and are full parties to the agreement, while the agent simply acts on behalf of the author who is signing the agreement. The agent is not a signatory, but is mentioned specifically in the preamble to the agreement and in the agency clause as their role will be relevant to actions in various clauses, such as the receiving of payments and finished copies on the author's behalf.

Note that if the author, estate or copyright owner has a company which is to be the relevant party in the agreement there will be variations on wording referencing the author and copyright owner later in the contract. A publisher may also require a separate inducement letter which obliges the author signing on behalf of their registered company to take on the obligations of the author.

The preamble gives the proposed title of the work covered by the agreement and briefly identifies the scope of the work in terms of genre, subject matter and number of pages, though this will be expanded on in the delivery clause later. If there is no agreed working or final title, and the work is described as "untitled," this brief description is important in terms of later identification of which work the contract pertains to. Sometimes a copy of a brief paragraph or fuller proposal will be appended to a contract and referred to here.

The preamble also offers clarity by indicating how various references will be made in the agreement, for example, "the Work," "the Author," "the Publisher" or "the Agent."

The preamble is important and administratively efficient because the negotiation partners can establish some key points of the agreement at a glance on the first page. In situations where there are other agreements between the parties (and more may be likely in the future), the preamble is useful in avoiding confusion regarding the work in question.

4.2 Effective date, term and earlier agreements

The contract must specify its term of validity, its relationship with earlier contracts and the date when it takes effect and becomes binding to the parties. Sometimes contracts are executed or signed by the parties after the effective date and, in such situations, the stipulated effective date applies. However, it is best practice to ensure that contracts are drawn and signed by both parties before commencement of work. Publishers and authors may have entered into earlier agreements, and it is important to indicate in this clause that the new agreement supersedes the earlier agreements. The agreement must also specify the term of the agreement, where the contract is not linked to an open arrangement (for instance, the full term of copyright or as long as the work sells at a certain rate). For example, the contract may run for a period of five, seven, ten or more years from the effective date and in such a case there may be provision to renew.

4.3 The grant of rights

The grant of rights is one of the central clauses in the contract. It follows the preamble and outlines the grant of publishing rights to the publisher, also known as primary or volume rights. This is the right to publish the author's work, which the author licenses to the publisher. These are the rights to print, produce and distribute copies of the book in key formats – in accordance with certain parameters of exclusivity or non-exclusivity, language, territory and term. Volume rights are the core rights exploited directly by the primary rights holder, the publisher, as opposed to subsidiary or secondary rights (which will be covered later). In the latter case, the publisher acquires certain ancillary rights, not necessarily to produce themselves, but with the intention of sublicensing these rights on to others, sharing revenue with the author.

Authors and their agents need to think carefully about the rights that they want to license to the publisher and those that they want to – and are able to – retain to sell independently of the publisher, whether via an agent or not. Similarly, the publisher also needs to think carefully about the rights that they want to license from the author. The parties need to consider which rights are best managed together for the benefit of both author and the publisher, enabling the publisher to promote the work effectively. It may take some negotiation to reach a satisfactory arrangement, since there may be differences of opinion on who should control certain elements of the author's IP at this stage, and what the resulting split of income should be. This is where appropriate minimum terms agreements can provide good guidelines and where contractual boilerplates between individual parties are helpful.

As discussed above, publishers should avoid insisting on rights that they have no intention of exploiting or where they lack proper means to do so, while also ensuring that they secure the rights they believe are critical to the effective exploitation of the work for mutual benefit.

A currently much-contested question in some markets is whether audio rights should be considered volume rights, rather than listed as subsidiary rights. Audio rights have often been retained by authors for separate sale to audio publishers with their own studios and narration expertise, similar to the licensing of film and television rights (see Section 4.15.13). There is pressure from publishers to automatically include audio rights in all publishing agreements, but audiobooks are not yet widely popular in all markets and not all publishers have the capacity to produce their own audiobooks, so they would simply license on to the same producers as authors would (but with a smaller percentage of the revenue going to the author).

Whatever rights are granted, to safeguard the author and their investment in their IP creation there should be a time limit for the publisher to exercise certain rights. If they fail to fulfill the commitment to produce a format in the stipulated time, the rights should revert to the author, rather than lying fallow.

Next, we will consider the key facets that must be established at the outset for a clear understanding of the shape and scope of the volume rights granted. These include where, how and for how long the publisher may publish the work and whether they are the only publisher who may do so in the territory and language.

4.3.1 Exclusivity and non-exclusivity

"Exclusivity" means that the rights are granted to the publisher alone, with no competing party, so that in a specific territory or for a specified period, only the contracting publisher can legally exploit those rights. When it comes to distribution, some markets may be demarcated as non-exclusive, meaning that more than one publisher can distribute and sell an edition into that market. For example, North American and UK publishers might both distribute their English language editions into certain European or Asian markets, unless otherwise specified.

4.3.2 Language and territory

Language rights refer to the language the publisher may publish in or license others to publish in. Unsurprisingly, language rights are closely allied to the question of territory, but with numerous differing contractual permutations, as rich and complex as the nature of human community, settlement, storytelling and commerce itself.

Publishers operate from within and across geographical markets and, along with language, territorial details need to be spelled out clearly at the start of the contract, indicating whether the license granted is limited to a country or region, or extends to the whole world. Even within a single originating language grant, some publishers may be entirely locally focused, with no distribution reach outside their country or region, while others may have a global footprint, either via the direct physical presence of their company or sister companies abroad, or through access to independent local partners. Authors who are asked for more than local publication rights to their work in the originating language must consider the potential reach that the publisher has into international same-language markets. As with many aspects of publishing there is no one-size-fits-all ideal: it depends on author, content, publisher and both parties' networks, via agents and publishing partners. Similar questions would pertain for an Angolan-Portuguese writer considering primary publication in Angola, Portugal or Brazil, as with a French-Canadian writer and the world Francophone market, or a Nigerian author writing in English considering offers from local or international English-language publishers.

The territory and language aspects of the rights granted clause work in tandem and there are many different combinations possible. If the territory granted is "world" (either in the English language or in all languages – WEL or WAL) there is no need for a detailed breakdown in an appendix or territory schedule. But where a country or region is granted, for instance Australia and New Zealand (ANZ), India or Southern Africa or United Kingdom and British Commonwealth rights (including or excluding Canada, according to negotiation) then there would be both a mention of the category or region in the rights granted clause and a reference to an appendix or territory schedule at the end of the contract. A similar principle would apply to contracts governing languages such as French, Portuguese or Spanish, covering the entire world in that language, versus a contract that is for WAL. This helps to avoid confusion or dispute over particular territories. It is important to clarify the territories in detail at negotiation stage and spell out the list in the contract, especially where the contract does not follow an established precedent between parties.

Where other languages beyond the language of origin are granted, the exercise of these secondary or "foreign" language rights usually involves a translation-rights-income split listed under the subsidiary rights clause. These may grant rights for other languages in the home territory, or for translation in international territories. Again, authors must consider the publisher's expertise for translation and payment of royalties, or sale into other languages as a sub rights sale, before granting or deciding to retain the language rights, usually for an agent to sell directly on the author's behalf.

On the other hand, publishers with capacity and reach who are active in international markets will seek to obtain more language rights and the overall deal value and other negotiation discussions will determine the outcome. Arrangements may also be reached where the publisher is granted limited time to exercise the right to sell a work in translation after which any unsold translation rights may revert to the author.

Where they have a choice, it is important for authors to match the manner of licensing of their work to the right publisher, in terms of this reach and expertise. Authors of works that are hyper-locally focused and do not have realistic prospects in other territories may not need publishers that have a global profile. Authors of works that have a broader geographical and cultural appeal will need publishers with physical presence or ability to take the work to other markets, or an agent to sell rights in different territories and languages. Literary agents are, by nature, global in outlook and tend to work with many partnering co-agents to sell authors' work to publishers in different parts of the world.

While some publishers may insist they need a global grant of rights, there is merit for authors in splitting territorial rights. It is often possible to separate out different regional rights within English-language publishing. For instance:

- An Indian or Nigerian author may sell publishing rights in their home territory to a local publisher, not as part of the grant to a US or UK publisher.
- French-Canadian and French rights in mainland Europe or continental Africa may be sold separately.
- Portuguese publishing rights may be sold separately in Angola or Mozambique versus Portuguese rights in Portugal or Brazil, or one publisher could control all Portuguese rights and manage the export of copies.
- Spanish rights can be carved up differently in Spain, the United States, Mexico, Argentina and other countries.

The options can be as varied as the countries and the consumers.

If handled well, a more granular regional approach can help to ensure robust, author-focused local publishing, marketing and publicity, and also more territories where the author earns home royalties, where such sales are possible. Local editions can also be more sensitively edited for the local market and suitably priced by a locally based publisher than editions printed at an international hub, with an export edition sold at a higher price due to print and distribution costs. Publication of a local edition can also provide more opportunity for promotion and events in an author's home market.

It can still be advisable, even if WAL rights are granted to a publisher, to have an agent to ensure the base contract allows authors to retain the necessary rights, or that reasonable sub rights splits are applied, as well as to monitor ongoing sales efforts. In the absence of an agent, authors' unions can often advise on contracts and the spread of language, territory and subsidiary rights that it is sensible to grant.

4.3.3 Term of contract: full term of copyright (FTOC) or fixed-term agreements

It should be pointed out here that the term of contract should not simply be conflated with the length of the protection of IP: a contract could be for 5 or 10 years only and does not necessarily need to encompass the FTOC (the life of the author +50 or +70 years, depending on the applicable legal framework).

As a matter of principle, every publication has a differing (and sometimes unpredictable) life cycle, from the time it is written and published to the time when demand for it ceases or reduces so that there is little point in continuing to make the work available. Throughout this process, reprints, new editions and other variations of the work may be issued. The term of copyright, where the exclusive rights apply and the work is protected, is usually a matter of national law. All contracts, but especially FTOC contracts, where legally permissible, need to include reversion parameters for when the work is no longer made available or sold in sufficient quantities to warrant continuation of the contract in terms of what delivers fair remuneration for the author.

In some countries reversion of rights is governed by law and in such cases parties to the contract are required to comply with the law.

However, publishers and authors (whether via an agent or not) can also agree to limit the term of the agreement from the outset. This could be 5, 7 or 10 years or whatever period they mutually agree to. The fixed-term agreement, which may be renewable according to an agreed process, is determined by several factors. These include the performance expectation, the nature of the work and the future plans of the author. However, as with other rights, some publishers may not be keen on fixed-term contracts, especially for work that has enduring potential where they would wish to recoup the investment made in producing the work over as long a period as legally possible.

Fixed-term contracts are more common in translation markets, for audio rights or for the onward sale of paperback rights. They are also common in the originating language with smaller publishers where authors may be reluctant to commit to a FTOC contract (where these are permissible) without assurance of strong publication. On the other hand, publishers may be reluctant to invest money, time and effort on works whose longer-term future performance income may not accrue to them. Authors may thus find the range of good publishers available to them is limited by a fixed-term restriction. As always, the expectations of author and publisher must be negotiated to mutual satisfaction and terms covering likely eventualities clearly laid out in the contract as far as possible. This includes reversions based on performance to safeguard IP income in all contracts, including FTOC contracts.

4.3.4 Volume form definition

Volume rights in all print formats are usually controlled by the originating publisher, often along with e-book rights, and these will be included in the volume rights definition. In most parts of the world, paperback editions (of varying sizes) traditionally constitute the primary reading format, with hardbacks sold as special editions in particular situations for top sellers. However, in some large markets, such as the United States, the United Kingdom, Germany and others, it is common for a hardback edition to be published first, often alongside the e-book, and then followed some months or a year (and sometimes more) later by the paperback. In some markets the larger (sometimes called C-format) trade paperback is produced at the same time as the hardback as a more affordable export edition, with a smaller (B- or A-format) paperback produced later.

Simultaneous print and e-book publishing is increasingly the norm in many larger book markets and what readers generally expect. But authors should be careful not to grant "enhanced" or "enriched" e-books, with additional audio or visual material, without explicit approval or an additional contractual arrangement. Such a digital enhancement license may lead to conflicts with potential audio and film deals later. Despite early enthusiasm for the possibilities of enhanced e-books and apps, this is not an area that even very large publishers have profitably focused on.

The right to print may include the right to produce POD editions. POD technology has improved markedly and proved vital during the distribution difficulties of the COVID-19 pandemic lockdowns. However, authors may wish to include a proviso that the quality should be equivalent to traditional hardback and paperback formats. They may also wish to request a sample copy of such POD or short print runs. Likewise, it should be ensured that the rights revert to the author if the sales of printed works fall below a specified minimum number within a certain fixed period. It can be stipulated in the contract that POD, if allowed, should not replace a first full print run, to ensure adequate print numbers and placement in libraries or bookshops.

As discussed, audio rights are sometimes included in the grant of rights to the main print publisher. But this is a matter for negotiation and can depend on the publisher and their production and sales capacity. In the past, publishers produced abridged audio editions due to the high cost of physical-format cassettes and CDs. More recently, digitization means that almost all audio deals are now unabridged audio recordings, for both the trade and library markets. In some large and more prosperous markets where consumers have vigorously adopted audiobooks, the audio editions may be published simultaneously or close to initial print and e-book publication. As audiobooks have different production processes it is advisable to have a separate clause covering audio rights (see also Section 4.14.4).

4.3.5 No abridgment or extract agreement

To protect the author's work, there should be a simple statement in the contract to say that no abridgment of the work shall be issued without their consent. This is usually followed by a proviso allowing the publisher to include a limited number of words or overall percentage of the book for publicity and marketing purposes and that any such extract will include a copyright line and full credit to the author.

A summary of a work is a different expression of the same idea and is generally not protected, depending on the jurisdiction. However, copyright on a summary that is substantial and contains significant chunks of verbatim material from the original belongs to the author. The publisher needs to agree with the author if they wish to produce summaries. This consideration also depends on the purpose of the summary:

- If it is used by the publisher to generate additional revenue, it is essential to seek agreement from the author and appropriate compensation needs to be agreed.
- If it is for promotional purposes in a clearly set framework, payment does not accrue to the author, unless the author undertook a specific action within the promotion action plan.

It is best, even for summaries that are meant for promotional use, to consult the author and gain approval for the summary wording and its intended use.

4.3.6 Subsequent editions

In educational and academic publishing, in particular, there is often a need to produce adapted or revised editions of a text, with the aim of extending the life of the work through relevant updates. For instance, with textbooks, this could be a response to changes in the curriculum and education requirements. A new edition might be desirable because the publisher is moving into other segments of the market. Here examples might include educational editions of general books or literature adapted for educational purposes. In these cases, some contracts might provide for the consent and participation of the author in the process, sometimes with a further advance to the author, depending on the initial negotiation agreement. Whether a further advance is involved or not, authors must decide if they want to have a say in the development of these new editions and publishers must be allowed to produce them effectively and in a timely manner. Thus, this clause often provides for consultation with the author and stipulates that such permission will not be unreasonably delayed or withheld. The clause often provides for the contribution and obligation of both parties, including the requirement for the author to update the information in the case of education, non-fiction or academic books. The author should be given enough time to update and provide the required material and be remunerated accordingly.

In certain cases, if the author is unable to provide the update, the publisher may contract another author to do so. The publisher may require the original author to share their future royalties with the contributor or to have the contributor's fees deducted from their future royalties. All these provisions must be captured in this clause. Future editions are meant to prolong and improve earnings for the author and the publisher, therefore, the same spirit of mutual interest should inform the engagement of both parties. Expectations of author time spent on revisions should be reasonable, along with the consideration of appropriate remuneration. Publishers should involve the authors in the process, seek their consent and reach appropriate agreement.

Depending on the amount of new material contributed by the substitute author in the new edition, the original author may have to agree to have the fee for the substitute author deducted from their own future earnings. In situations where the substitute author's work is substantial or replaces the original author's work, the original author may have to share their royalties with the substitute author. However, they must be credited in subsequent editions and compensated for their original concept. As indicated earlier, where applicable, publishers must ensure that the contract allows them to continue with the work when some of the authors can no longer continue contributing.

The contractual requirement for authors to update subsequent editions is not relevant to fiction, and less relevant to general trade non-fiction. In these areas it would be customary for any additional material, such as a fresh introduction, to be subject to a new fee, by mutual agreement. Authors may, for instance, be asked to write new introductions to works of classic literature. Updating subsequent editions remains largely of concern in educational and academic publishing and in some general non-fiction by specifically negotiated contractual agreement.

4.4 Author's warranties and indemnities

The author is responsible for the work they submit to the publisher. They should give the publisher guarantees that it is their own original work, that it does not libel other parties and it does not infringe the authors' rights or copyright of any other work. The author guarantees that any facts purporting to be true are indeed true. This clause requires the author to provide these guarantees and to indemnify the publisher from any legal action or costs that may result from the author breaching these warranties. Some publishers' insurance policies require language in this clause that can be quite onerous for the author and it is a clause that needs to be carefully scrutinized and implications understood. If possible, the author should only be liable for sustained breaches, not just breaches that are alleged, though there will be limits to what clause changes may be made in some cases.

It is important that, in addition to this clause, the publisher is thorough in ensuring that the material is not an infringement of existing work, that it is original and that it is not libelous. Publishers can use software to check the originality of work, but they should always carefully discuss the work with authors and seek legal opinion where they suspect that material may be libelous.

Publishers and authors must also be mindful of variation in laws in the different countries in which copies may be sold – more than one legal read may be needed in this case, one for each relevant territory's legal system.

Due to the development of AI, large language models (LLMs) and automatic text generators, some publishers are now also seeking contractual assurances that the text was created by the author, without the aid of a text generator. They may also seek assurance from authors that they have written it in accordance with the nationally applicable laws on the personal level of creation – in other words, that they wrote it themselves. This has important implications for future claims to remuneration, including, where applicable, collective rights management.

In complementary fashion, new contractual language is being worked out framing publishers' assurances to authors regarding the limits of AI use in their publishing processes, also that any such use be deployed only within closed systems, along with guarantees that the publisher will not allow any text and data scraping and use of the authors' copyright work. Along with legal challenges linked to the development of LLMs using copyright material, it will take some time for AI-linked clause language to be settled in a way satisfactory to the relevant parties.

4.5 Author's reserved rights

The author may be able to negotiate to withhold certain rights and not to grant them to the publisher and there may be rights not yet defined which may become relevant in the future. While some specifically excluded rights may be specified in this clause, it is best to simply state clearly that the rights that are not explicitly granted are reserved by the author. It is also no longer customary to license the too-broad "unknown types of use," which has sometimes been included in the past. It also makes sense, in part as protection for the publisher's investment too, to clearly state that the author's work may not be used in text and data mining (TDM) for generative AI purposes, as a safeguard if the author-created copyright text and IP in the work are used illegally in large-scale language models without consent or compensation.

4.6 Author's delivery: text length, illustrations, photos, permissions, index

While the preamble gives a snapshot description of the work, the delivery clause goes into more detail about the extent and scope of the work, including the required number of (standard) pages or words in the manuscript. This clause also specifies the additional materials to be delivered, including text, permissions for any copyright material by others to be included, illustrations and index, if required. All this information is an essential aid to the publisher's planning and budgeting. In some cases, at the time of negotiation it should be agreed whether the publisher will cover all or some of the costs for images, maps or index, or how such costs will be shared. It is common for authors to apply for, pay and confirm textual permissions but, again, this can be negotiable depending on text, publisher or author. An example could be a literary biography where many quotations may have to be cleared via the copyright holder, which is often a literary estate. If a legal read is required, this clause should specify the details of payment. Often this is shared 50/50 by publisher and author.

A crucial element of this clause is the delivery date, which must be a realistically achievable date, mutually agreed. Depending on the target market, an author missing the delivery date can lead to late publication of the work, with major consequences. This can be especially relevant when the book is part of a promotional program or campaign by retailers, or is required for submission to education authorities, as in the case of textbooks. The publisher and the author must agree on all these elements and the author must ensure that the required manuscript is delivered on time and to the agreed specifications. Equally the publisher should respond to the manuscript with editorial notes in a timely manner. The delivery clause is particularly sensitive because the context of late-delivery situations can vary greatly: for instance, if the author chooses not to deliver the work at all, it is fair to expect the author to pay back the advance to the publisher. However, a situation can also depend on the degree of breach of the author, who might not be able to deliver in a timely fashion when, for instance, a publisher gives slow or incomplete feedback.

The clause also requires the author to retain copies of the materials that have been delivered, either physically or electronically. This is important to both the author and the publisher in the event of the materials being lost or damaged.

If the author does not deliver the materials in the format specified in the agreement, for example, the correct electronic format, or with a required index, the publisher may proceed to convert the text or generate the index accordingly. The clause may provide for the deduction of the cost of such work from the author's future earnings, rather than the author being directly invoiced up front. However, the publisher needs to give the author a fair and reasonable opportunity to provide these materials before bringing in any external contributor.

4.7 Publisher's acceptance or decision not to publish

Just as the author commits to a delivery date, the publisher also commits to a specific time period in which the book will be published (see Section 4.9.1). This could be either the seasonal program and year, or within a certain number of months of delivery and acceptance of the manuscript, and publication payment is usually linked to this time period.

The publisher may nevertheless not be able to publish, or may refuse to go ahead with a publication if the author has not delivered according to the agreement or after an agreed date has been missed without good reason, especially in the case of particularly time-sensitive or event-related books. When this happens, the author should be free to pursue opportunities with other publishers (or to self-publish). Depending on the contract, some publishers may require the author to pay back some or all of the advance payments made to them so far, but if non-publication is not due to a breach on the author's part, there should be no requirement for repayment, even if the author chooses to publish elsewhere. Some clauses of this type can be very extensive, going into great detail about how it is to be determined that a manuscript is inadequate, below standard or unpublishable and where responsibility for non-publication lies.

Care must be taken by both parties to ensure they have sufficient protections and remedies here if things go wrong at delivery stage. Both will already have invested time, effort and money in the project and stand to lose a great deal through non-delivery or non-publication.

4.8 Editing, author's corrections and proofs

One of the key responsibilities of the publisher is to edit the work, suggesting changes and providing corrections to the text submitted by the author. The publisher must always consult with the author, who is required to respond to the edit and copy-edit, and then to read, check and correct the proofs within the stipulated time. If the author does not correct the proofs in this period, the publisher can assume that the changes are approved for press and proceed with only the in-house or freelance proofreader's input. This clause ensures that there is no misunderstanding between the author and the publishers on the final ready-for-press material and that the publishing process is not held back by the author's delays.

The clause may also limit the number of changes that the author may make in the proof files by stipulating that if these changes are above a certain agreed proportion of the text, the publisher is entitled to deduct attendant costs from the author's future royalty earnings. While it is necessary and desirable for the author to make corrections to the proofs, frivolous or repeated rounds of corrections can delay the publication. This clause is meant to reduce the amount of time spent on the work at proof stage and the resulting cost of doing so. Again, where editorial disputes arise, this is where a good relationship guided by mutual interest and respect can resolve issues effectively beyond the details the contract governs.

4.9 Publication: time frame, format, design and promotion

This clause stipulates the responsibilities and obligation of the parties regarding the aspects specified below. This is meant to ensure that parties understand their responsibilities and obligations and to prevent future disagreements over these issues.

4.9.1 Time frame for publication

The agreement requires the publisher to publish within a certain period, usually either from the date of the signature of the contract or from delivery of the text, as stated in the contract. It also requires that they will publish further formats in a manner linked to original publication timing. It also stipulates that the agreement will terminate if the publisher does not publish within the designated time. The provision is meant to protect the author from delays by the publisher. Such delays may be detrimental to the author in many ways, including potential reputational damage and lost income. The author should insist on this clause to enable them to receive due remuneration and pursue other opportunities in a timely fashion if the publisher cannot go ahead with the publication.

4.9.2 Format: hardback, paperback, e-book, audio

The clause stipulates the planned formats for the publication and acts to forestall any dispute or disappointment at the time of publication. The publisher may insist on the right to determine the format, as they are responsible for the promotion, packaging, distribution and selling of the book. However, this must be in line with the rights granted. Where audio rights have also been granted to the publisher, whether for their own production or licensing on, mention of this format should also be made here. This should include a clause allowing for reversion of rights if no audio edition is planned in a timely fashion to coincide with print publication (or close to print publication) as is customary when the publisher has acquired audio rights in their deal.

4.9.3 Title, cover, description: consultation and approval

The design and presentation of a book is determined by the publisher as part of their responsibility for marketing and selling the work, though publishers must consult and seek agreement from the author. Wording here may grant approval on some aspects, such as the title, and approval or consultation on others, such as the cover design and cover and catalogue copy. For a positive publication, collaboration between author and publisher is crucial. Publishers will ensure the cover is approved by their marketing department and may also often need the approval of larger retailers in competitive bookselling markets. While the publisher retains the ultimate responsibility for these elements, authors can make a huge contribution to effective publicity and marketing. Authors will more enthusiastically support the promotion of work when they are satisfied with all aspects of the presentation, including important aspects such as the title and cover of the book. In authors' rights legislation countries, collaboration and confirmation of such details with the author are necessary as any resulting negative impact to the author could mean a violation of moral rights.

4.9.4 Author promotion, approved biography and photographs

Authors need to provide biographical information for the generation of promotional materials, press releases, catalogs, website, book jackets and data feeds to retailers. This clause requires the author to consent to the use of the author's name, agreed biographical details and approved likeness in the promotion of the book. In principle, author photos are usually the responsibility of the publisher, since not only production but also (remunerated) transfer of rights for the use of the image, to which the photographer holds the copyright, are necessary. Sometimes, however, authors have author pictures produced at their own expense and buy the rights in order to maintain control. In this case, contractual agreements between photographer-author-publisher on rights of use, territories and limits are required.

4.9.5 Marketing materials and proposed retail price

The publisher is responsible for the promotion and selling of the work and as such retains the right to set the price of the book and to negotiate discounts to retailers and wholesalers. They are also responsible for all the relevant metadata and for generating marketing assets, such as advertisements, point-of-sale display materials, and additional visual assets used on e-retailing platforms and social media. The author needs to be informed of the retail price and of discount levels, where relevant. It is best practice to share marketing materials with the author and involve them in the development of such materials.

4.10 Return of manuscript and other materials belonging to the author

The manuscript and other materials such as photographs and illustrations submitted by the author remain the property of the author and this clause records what will happen to the material after publication. In some cases, the publisher will dispose of the material and in others the author may insist on their return - this must be agreed to before the publishing process begins. The publisher can include a clause to say that they are not responsible in the event of loss of materials, and some may insist that postage and insurance costs for the return of materials are to be borne by the author. It is advisable for authors to keep a copy of all their materials when they deliver to publishers, whether in hard copy or digitally.

4.11 Copyright notice

Every contract for book publication should stipulate the format of the copyright notice including the author's name and the year of first publication. There will be varieties of copyright wording for estates and for authors who use registered companies or write under pseudonyms. Copyright law also differs between countries, so it is important to be familiar and comply with the specific and applicable national law.

With co-authored, translated and illustrated books, there should also be copyright notices for the co-authors, translators and illustrators. For an anthology there would be a separate copyright notice for the editor, both regarding any introduction, if written by the editor, and the assembling of the material, with individual short story, poem or essay copyrights noted for the contributors. Sometimes there will be a summary copyright notice for contributors on the copyright page and fuller details listed at the back of the anthology.

4.12 Moral rights and changes to the work

Moral rights are authors' rights linked to copyright, concerning the connection between authors and their work:

- the author's right to be identified as the originator of the work (the right of attribution, sometimes called "paternity"); and
- the author's right to control or prevent "derogatory treatment of the work" - that is, changes to the work which might damage or distort their reputation (the "right of integrity").

This means that copies of their work, in all formats, should carry their chosen name at all times (whether that is the author's real name, pseudonym or decision to remain anonymous) in a visible manner (on the front cover). The work and its wording may also not be altered without the author's consent, or in ways with which they do not wish to be associated. Though moral rights are often not asserted, publishers should respect authors' moral rights as this retains the integrity of the work and maintains respect and good relationships between publishers and authors.

Linked to these is the moral right of false attribution (a crucial issue, for instance, on books put together with AI-generated content): the right not to have a work wrongly attributed to you. This could cause reputational damage, for instance, when a new edition of a work is published that fundamentally changes the original work and is not approved by the author. Moral rights are also applicable to translators of the original work. An additional right (also covered in stronger privacy laws in many countries these days) is the right of privacy: the right not to have photos or films which were commissioned for private use issued to the public.

The rights mentioned above are automatic, apart from the right of attribution which, in some countries, must be specifically asserted by the author, which is why this clause is advisable in contracts in certain jurisdictions. In some jurisdictions, for example, a statement about the author asserting their moral rights should be included along with the copyright notice on the copyright page of the published book.

Moral rights are perpetual. Under South African copyright law, however, moral rights do not have to be asserted and a clause doing so is not necessary in contracts where the book is only published in South Africa.

Moral rights pass to an author's heirs or the holder of their copyright upon their death. During the author's life, moral rights cannot be sold or transferred to another party like economic rights, but may (in some but not all jurisdictions) be waived by the author, where, for instance, a license requires extensive changes to the text. Here are some examples of situations where moral rights may be waived:

- A ghost writer might waive the right to be identified as the author of the ghostwritten text.
- For extracts or serialization in magazines or newspapers, or when an author licenses a theater, musical or film version of their work, a moral rights waiver will be required by the producers. This is because changes will be inevitable in the development of the script and production of the work and cannot be individually approved by an author.
- A moral rights waiver would be seen where a purchaser is seeking an assignment of copyright rather than a license.

Note that in authors' rights legislation, for example in France, an author can always change their mind on the waiver and require the inclusion of their name on the publication later.

Moral rights are protected in slightly differing ways via the laws of many countries. In the United States, only the Visual Artists Rights Act of 1990 provides limited moral rights protections to creators of visual art works, in specific conditions. In most countries, including France, all authors are holders of moral rights.

4.13 Advance payments

Authors need a financial advance for the exploitation of their work, as a great deal of personal investment is made before a share of revenue is realized from the sale of the book. Authors have often already made extensive inputs in terms of research and writing before an agreement is signed with the publisher. Calculation of the appropriate advance payment to the author depends on the publisher's estimation of their prospects of recouping the money from the sales of the work later. Royalties and any other payments that become due to the author in the future from sub rights will be set against the guaranteed advance, until the full level of advance is paid out. Then further payments due will be paid within a certain period, as laid out in the accounting clause of the contract.

An advance and its value illustrate the publisher's confidence and commitment to the work, and will be affected by genre, topicality, author reputation and whether there is competition for the author's work. Payment of advances should be standard practice, but there is variation for certain genres which can be riskier in terms of income, especially over the short to medium term. This also varies for digital-first publishing models, where a contract may be agreed for no advance, but the royalty share is higher. Common practice varies greatly in less-developed markets, according to genre, author profile and size of publisher. The publisher may insist on putting the full risk on the author by not paying an advance. In all cases, the actual long-term earnings via the royalty share is key. In some countries, for example in France, advance payments are mandatory if the publisher does not disclose the number of copies in the first print run in the contract.

Advance payments may be scheduled in varying ways in the author–publisher agreement. In some advance formats, particularly for smaller deals or for secondary language or translation contracts, the entire amount may be paid on signature. Half-signature, half-delivery payments are also common, though alternative arrangements may be reached during negotiation. Another option is payment in thirds, making a payment incentive for satisfactory delivery, as follows:

- On signature by both parties: the publisher requires the author to commit to the project by signing the contract and when the commitment commences the author should receive at least a first portion of payment.
- On delivery of work: the next common milestone is the delivery of the work to the publisher's specification as defined in the contract. This is an incentive for the author to complete and submit an acceptable work on time.
- On publication or within a certain period (for instance, 12 months) from signature (if the book is already delivered) or delivery (if the book is still being written when the contract is signed). Good wording might stipulate that the advance is paid on publication, when the publisher can begin to generate revenue from the book, or one year from the signature of the contract, whichever is the sooner. This is to protect the author from slow or late payment due to publication delay on the publisher's part. For this a proposed publication date should be stipulated in the contract, as discussed earlier.
- There may be additional bonus advances if the book reaches a certain bestseller status, quantified via parameters such as official chart position or number of copies sold within a certain period. These are therefore calculated at an appropriate time after publication when the relevant figures are available. A book which is made into a film or television series might receive a broadcast or screening bonus when it reaches film theaters or television screens. However, this clause would usually limit the triggering of this bonus to broadcast linked to a defined list of major channels or key streamers.

Many publishers would seek in their own cashflow interests to spread advance payments out as far as possible, while authors would argue for faster payments for their work. In markets where multiple formats are common, some publishers push for four payments, to include signature, delivery, first publication (often hardback or trade paperback) and delay a final payment to paperback formats. These are all matters for individual negotiation and individual arrangements, and exceptions can always be made.

4.13.1 Multiple book deals: separate or joint accounting

Where a contract is for multiple books, especially for linked or series titles, the publisher may wish to spread their risk by asking for joint accounting with the earn-out on the total advance spread over several titles. On the other hand, authors and their agents will seek to ensure that success is rewarded book by book and to ensure that any royalties earned above the advance for the first book will be paid over sooner rather than later. Again, this is a matter for individual negotiation. Joint accounting is less favorable for the author and is forbidden in some countries, such as France, unless applied at the request of the author.

4.14 Royalties

While the royalty clauses relate to the publisher's own editions sold, both in the local "home" market and in export territories, in some cases the publisher may consider licensing formats on to other parties. These options are covered in the subsidiary rights section (see Section 4.15). There is always a set of strategic choices and an interplay between the direct sales of publisher-produced material and subsidiary rights licensed on to others. In principle the author should be informed before any license is concluded and their consent is recorded.

The same contract may have audio rights included under the royalties section as well as the subsidiary rights section, to cover both possibilities, depending on whether the publisher chooses to produce their own edition or license on. As a result, there will be some repetition of information in this royalties section and the subsidiary rights section below.

The protection of sound or audio recordings differs according to jurisdictions; in some jurisdictions they are treated as separate copyright work.

In some cases, a flat-rate royalty may be offered for a format or edition, but it is common to see rising royalties, also known as stepped, staggered or escalating royalties. These increase by certain percentages after a designated number of sales. All of these levels will be subject to negotiation for different authors and projects and may differ between formats. In Europe, under recent directives, flat rates or total buy-out lump sums are the exception, as they are in conflict with the principle of a proportional and appropriate remuneration.

It is also important to understand what the royalty percentage is based on. This can make a great difference to actual income, so it is important to clearly understand the figures and possible sums that are being offered or accepted.

- A royalty rate may be based on the published price (or "recommended retail price"), which is the price the publisher has set. Alternatively, in some countries, this may be secured by a fixed book price system. This fixed price is sometimes marked on the physical copy, where applicable.
- Alternatively, the royalty could be based on net receipts (or "price received"), meaning the actual amounts received by the publisher after discounts to retailers.
- Within the same contract, some royalties may be made on published price, others on net receipts. E-book royalties, for instance, are often calculated on net receipts because of the rising discounts and provisions of the online marketplace and pricing variation.

Across the print formats mentioned in the following sections, there are likely to be variations on the main "home market" royalties (linked to the exclusive territory, as discussed in Section 4.3 "The grant of rights"). These variations include a lower royalty level for copies exported beyond the home market and pre-agreed adjustments to the standard royalty rate. This allows the publisher to pay the author a lower royalty when they are selling copies at higher discount levels, usually applicable to higher order numbers (in countries with no fixed book prices). These clauses have, in regions without a fixed book price system, become more prominent and vigorously debated as the power of major retail chains, supermarkets and internet retailers has grown, accompanied by greater and more compelling demands for deep discounting. Some contracts in these regions may allow for a "special sales" clause, for sales outside of normal retail channels, with author approval of the deal, though these may also be covered by a "high discount" clause. In addition to the major retailers' discounted orders, examples of such high discount or special sales might include:

- specialist mail order catalogues or non-bookshop retail chains adding book stock to their offering; or
- a hotel or corporate business placing a large one-off order of a relevant title, for a special promotion, gift or conference content.

In some markets and under special legal exceptions, enormous unit sales can be achieved when a book is adopted on a school or university exam syllabus. The numbers involved in high-population countries will be huge, though the unit price and author royalty per copy may be low. It may be wise to have specific syllabus adoption terms noted in the contract at the outset in case the book is prescribed in this way. Otherwise, usual high-discount terms will apply. In some cases where a royalty figure cannot be agreed beforehand it is possible to settle at "to be mutually agreed" (TBMA) in the contract, to allow for a future negotiation regarding special circumstances at the time in which they occur.

4.14.1 Hardback

The hardback or hardcover, also known as cloth or case-bound cover, is made from thick cardboard that is cloth-wrapped, usually with an additional paper dust jacket. Hardbacks are more expensive to produce and are aimed at a more affluent market. They are less commonly produced in economically developing world markets due to the higher production and distribution costs, poor affordability and in some cases the effect of taxes on books. Some publishers might produce an initial paperback edition for their markets and produce a hardback only for very popular authors, for libraries or as a special edition. Special editions could be, for instance, for collectors, a certain retail chain or an anniversary.

Hardback royalties to an author in a general trade contract are often higher than the trade paperback or mass market royalties, though the expectation would be that fewer copies of the more expensive edition would be sold.

4.14.2 Paperback editions: trade and mass market

Paperback, pocketbook or softcover formats are less costly to produce than hardbacks, and so offer a less expensive option for the reader. There are varying sizes of paperback, with different terminology used in different markets. The larger (or C-format) trade paperback edition, often with flaps, in more expensive versions, is a preferred first publication format in many countries, especially for smaller publishers. The trade paperback format is usually preferred as first format in Australia and New Zealand, India, South Africa, Nigeria, Kenya, Egypt and other African countries and economically developing markets. As first format, trade paperback royalties may be closer to hardback royalties, though publishers would expect to sell the trade paperback in greater numbers.

Smaller format, second edition or mass market royalties may usually start at a lower percentage than the hardback or trade paperback, but would be the longest-lasting ongoing format, reaching the most readers. Sometimes the trade paperback and mass market royalties will be the same, or there will be no mass market editions produced. All of these factors are sensitive to readers' and retailers' demand, publisher capacity and author status, and also have escalator possibilities as per negotiation.

The sale of paperback rights to specialist paperback publishers used to be the norm, when some originating publishers produced only hardbacks. Today, publishing operates in a more "vertical" fashion format-wise, which means the same publisher starts with a hardback, and after a certain period, of months or years, a paperback is printed. However, paperback rights deals are still concluded between two publishers in certain situations. This is covered further under subsidiary rights below (see Section 4.15).

4.14.3 E-book

There is great variation across international e-book markets. In developed markets, print and electronic publication is almost always simultaneous and, in these cases, e-book rights are usually part of the main primary rights granted to the publisher. The e-book is usually an identical format to the print book, as opposed to a potentially enhanced or abridged digital version, which should be subject to separate agreement. In situations where the publisher does not have the capacity to issue an e-book edition, they may license it to an e-book specialist in their own territory. If e-book rights are handled separately from print rights, the author and the publisher must agree on the sublicensing arrangement as with all the other rights to third parties, such as e-book aggregators, and written consent by the author to the agreement should be required. E-book publication requires skill regarding both production and ongoing metadata management from the publisher.

E-book royalties have for some years been based on net receipts but at a much higher percentage figure than the print percentage based on published price (with escalator possibilities as per negotiation). Given the rapidly changing nature of the digital world, in trade publishing a clause agreeing to a review of the e-book royalty is common after an agreed period, such as two years.

In some markets, it is also common for authors to decide whether their e-book can be included in streaming or subscription programmes, or whether the publisher may license it for electronic lending in platforms of public libraries.

It is also becoming increasingly important to ask the author if he/she wants to opt out of text and data mining (TDM). In this way, a publisher can be sure to protect its investment while keeping open the option of sublicensing TDM if the law and the author permits.

4.14.4 Audio

Where the publisher has been granted audio rights to produce directly there will be an audio royalty in the contract. Like the e-book royalty, digital audiobook royalties are based on net receipts, with a higher percentage point than the figure for sale of physical copies. Commercial audio is now almost entirely focused on full, unabridged recordings for digital download or streaming, to be listened to on phones, computers and other devices. The costs for producing CDs of unabridged audio are high and libraries are, in some countries, the main outlet for physical goods in audio. As with e-books, there may be an audio review clause.

When deals are done directly with specialist audio publishers, these are usually on a fixed-term license, with the possibility of renewal on mutual agreement at the end of the term. These audio contracts would also be limited to specific territories and care must be taken to avoid a potential clash when licensing more than one contract in the same language but covering different territories.

However audio rights are produced and sold, whether abridged or unabridged, the license must be limited to a non-dramatized recording (often single-voice, though multiple voices may be permissible if it is not dramatized), so as not to conflict with radio dramatization and film rights deals. The author should have the right of approval or meaningful consultation over a choice of narrators. If the author narrates the audio, this should be subject to a separate performance fee. If a publisher acquires audio rights, there should be a commitment to publish simultaneously with, or close to, publication and there may be a provision to revert the rights should this not be done. Should a separate audio publisher acquire the rights, the author and their agent must ensure that the audio edition may not be released before the print publisher's edition.

Audio rights are an increasingly contested territory, with digital technology reducing the cost of audio for the consumer. This has made full, unabridged audio a more common format, especially for trade books, with agented authors and publishers both wishing to manage these rights. There are widespread concerns about streaming and subscription models and whether, as in the music industry, the creator receives fair remuneration from these models. As with any swiftly moving developments in the market, the publisher should seek to explain as much as possible to the author and seek agreement to the inclusion of the author's work on such platforms. Debates on this matter will continue in a dynamic and growing market. Technological developments such as AI-generated text to speech is also causing great concern for both authors and voice artists. Here, the author may wish to insist contractually on human voices, to maintain the integrity and credibility of their work.

As with e-book, in some markets authors may have the right of approval over their work's inclusion for digital audio lending in public libraries and on subscription and streaming programmes.

4.14.5 Translator fees or royalties

If the work is translated from another language, it is good practice for the translator to receive a fee per word or print page. Sometimes the translator may receive a percentage royalty in addition to a fee, though this would be a much smaller proportion than the royalty to the author (or often only after a minimum number of copies have already been sold). This would need to be stipulated in a separate contract with the translator but should be mentioned in the author's contract to ensure the author's consent is clear. Though not ideal and considered less fair on the author, sometimes the author will receive a lower royalty than if their work was written in the target language, to accommodate the translator royalty. In this case the author is effectively paying the translator through royalty sacrifice. In other cases, the translator royalty may be in addition to the author royalty, but these are matters for individual publisher-agent-author-translator negotiations. As a publisher or translator, it may be worthwhile to research translation grants that cover printing costs, for example, in order to avoid the costs of translation being covered by the original author's fee.

It is becoming increasingly important to develop appropriate contractual language to deal with machine translation challenges. In order to preserve the integrity of their work, authors can insist on wording that ensures their work is not translated using AI. Equally, translators must ensure that their translation has not been produced using AI so that they become "post-AI editors."

4.14.6 Free or promotional copies

Publishers may give away free copies as samples, for review and promotional activities, and for legal deposit as required by law (for example, to a national legal deposit or state library). No royalties are payable on such copies as the publisher receives no revenue. Both the author and the publisher may benefit from additional or better sales that come from the promotional activities and word-of-mouth generated, though such free copies should not be excessive so as to eat into the author's income. Therefore there is often an agreed cap on the number of such free copies in the contract. The publisher should be transparent about the number of free copies issued in the author's royalty statement details.

4.15 Subsidiary rights

Subsidiary rights, also referred to as secondary rights, sub rights or sublicenses, are a stage beyond primary or volume rights, though in some instances there can be some overlap. Strategic and negotiating choices are made as to which rights are retained by the author and which are granted to the publisher to further license to third parties, including to publishers in other territories. Subsidiary rights include but are not limited to audiobook and translation rights, other territory rights, book club rights, serial and other media.

Any rights not mentioned in the contract are to be retained by the author, as also stated in the separate reserved rights clause (see Section 4.5).

Some works may be adapted for specific interest groups, such as educational or children's editions. The publisher must make sure that such editions will indeed reach new markets and not disrupt or cannibalize the sales of the original edition. Authors will often require a clause stating they must give approval in the case of some adapted editions. In the case of specialized adaptations such as graphic novels, authors must be careful that these do not conflict with other visual or dramatic adaptation contracts they may enter into separately, such as film, theater and television. Further different formats are also meant for particular audiences, such as large print and Braille.

Publishing contracts should have a separate subsidiary rights clause, with subclauses for each right. These should spell out the income percentage split and indicate where author approval is necessary, and where the author and the publisher need to agree on the licensing to third parties. The contract usually specifies that the author may not unreasonably refuse to grant permission for such a rights sale. At this stage of the work's life cycle, with the work already written, edited and the primary copies selling, there is usually less additional investment on the part of the publisher beyond what is needed to make their own direct sales. As a result often a greater part of the incoming payment is paid to the author. The author's share is usually initially set against the author's advance amount, if this is not yet earned out, until such time as the author's income exceeds the advance amount.

Subsidiary rights splits may range between 50 percent and 90 percent to the author. Income from sub rights sales should be clearly shown on the author's royalty statements. The author should clarify whether the split they will receive is the full or gross amount received by the publisher and that there are no additional intermediary agents' fees or other fees (such as taxes or transportation fees) to be subtracted. Wording to this effect should be included in the contract. If a payment on a sub rights sale is to be made before the contractual royalty payment period or is not to be set against the advance, this is usually specifically negotiated in some form of "flow-through" clause. Swifter sub rights payment to authors may be requested for large amounts, such as major serial rights deals to a newspaper for a topical book, or when a UK publisher who has WEL rights licenses US rights to a US publisher, and vice versa.

To make sure that such opportunities are not lost to the publisher and the author, publishers must pass on offers to authors in a timely fashion and authors must respond promptly to such requests.

Publishers may want to secure as many rights as possible, including those that they may only exploit in the future. But they should not insist on rights that they know they are not likely to exploit, or where they do not have the means or competence to take appropriate action. As a safeguard, where there is debate around certain subsidiary rights, authors may suggest a limited time frame within which the publisher can exercise their exclusive right to sell these rights on. The time limit should be realistic and give the publisher reasonable time to exploit the rights. After the specified time, either the publisher and the author can negotiate an extension of the time to exploit the right, or the rights should revert to the author who can then find an agent to exploit the right (or they can exploit the right themselves).

4.15.1 First and second serial rights

Serial rights are extracts from a book that may be sold to different outlets, usually newspapers and magazines, online or in print, before or after the publication of the book. Serialization in magazines, newspapers and other publications and platforms can provide additional income as well as good publicity and advertising for the work in different spheres. This may lead to better sales and higher revenue for the publisher and the author. These rights may be controlled by the publisher or may be retained by the author, who may choose to work with an agent to place these strategically. Consultation with the publisher and their publicity department regarding the timing of publication of any extract is essential to maximize publicity without jeopardizing book sales.

The publisher and the author must also agree whether the publication or platform can allow other outlets to serialize as well and how strict any timing embargo or exclusivity period might be. Selling first serial rights, to take place before publication or on the date of the book's launch, is the most desirable for stimulating demand for the book. Second serialization takes place after publication of the work; both first and second serial rights can be licensed where there is strong interest in a title. First serial rights would usually be exclusive to one party, while second serial rights can be sold as many times as there is interest and agreement.

In practice, serial rights are tricky to place. Financial rewards tend to be lower in the digital age as opposed to when newspapers and magazines were print-only and did not face the competition of so much free content on social media. As newspapers' priorities can change swiftly with current events, it is advisable to agree a fixed "kill fee" if the publication secures exclusive first serial rights but decides not to publish at the last minute.

The bulk of the serial rights payment, as in most other subsidiary rights, would be assigned to the author. This might range between 75 percent and 90 percent for second and first serial respectively.

4.15.2 Editions in other territories

Publishers often distribute their own edition around the world where there is demand, physically moving the copies they print in the home country. They can also license third parties to publish, print and sell the work in other territories, especially those markets that the author or the publisher cannot reach effectively. In the case of English-language authors this might involve concluding separate sublicense deals for rights in territories such as the United States, Canada, Australia, New Zealand, Nigeria, India or Southern Africa.

This might comprise a fresh edition with a new cover, and additional materials such as an introduction, glossary or notes. Alternatively, the acquiring publisher might simply take over all the files (usually for a separate fee to the rights license, depending on negotiation) and print a similar copy, but to local specifications, depending on format preference, paper availability and other local preferences.

In some cases, the author may have retained the publishing rights to a particular market or region, especially if it is their home country or place of residence, if they have a chance of a separate publishing deal there. This is often the case in markets such as Australia, New Zealand, South Africa, Kenya, Nigeria and more. In this case, a separate deal for this market would be negotiated by the author or their agent.

4.15.3 Other format editions

Where publishers are not in the best position to capitalize on a hardback or paperback edition, but there is market demand, they may sell on certain format rights to another publisher in their market. This could be either for a special hardback edition or a mass market paperback. This might be desirable, for instance where the original publisher, often a small independent house, has released a book which becomes a success, but the publisher then finds they do not have the capacity to print and sell in the paperback quantities needed to meet demand, or a publisher realizes they are not able to reach wider export markets as efficiently. These editions would directly repeat the text of the original edition, possibly with the addition of extra material such as reading group notes, author foreword or an introduction by another writer. These format subsidiary rights would usually be retained by the publisher to avoid market confusion and competition between the formats, and so that timing can be strategically managed.

There can be wide variation, dependent on negotiation, in the author–publisher split for licensing on other original-language editions such as separate hardback and paperback in the publisher's own home territory or in part of their export market instead of distributing their own edition.

Technological advances mean publishers mostly have the capacity to publish and market their own e-book editions, though some contracts may include a provision to license on to a third party. This is far less common than in the past, and some contracts now dispense with an e-book sublicense clause entirely.

4.15.4 Translation rights

Translation rights are rights to publish in languages other than the original language and are sometimes known as "foreign language rights." These may be in the same geographical but multilingual territory as the originating publisher (as with India or countries on the African continent, or with Catalan language rights in Spain) or in other territories and languages further afield. In the same local territory, the originating publisher may also manage the translation into the other language(s). However, there may be specialist local publishers in the different languages and the author will have to weigh up the possibilities here according to context.

In other territories, translation rights are licensed for a fee to the translating publisher (usually for a fixed-term contract). The acquiring publisher will commission and manage the translation. Wherever translation rights are sold it is vital for the seller to secure a good publisher who will commission a competent (human, not AI) translator with an excellent understanding of both the source and target languages and cultures. This will ensure the translation has the necessary cultural and linguistic nuance for the translation market. The author or the publisher can do the necessary licensing depending on the contract, but good agents do this particularly well for their authors. If the author is also fluent in the target language, they may have consultation or approval over the resulting translation, with a balance between the author's wishes and the translator's wishes under their moral rights (both being owners of moral rights under the concerned legislations). As noted above, translators would have a separate contract with the publisher and can, above their fixed fee, also receive a royalty, which should ideally not be taken from the original author's royalty share.

4.15.5 Book club rights

Book club rights entail the bulk sale at large discounts to book clubs for resale to their members or in some cases licensing them the right to produce and print their own edition for their members. In the latter case, the publisher is not involved in the printing and distribution of the book, so about 50 percent to 60 percent or more of the fees paid by the book club to the publisher are paid on to the author. However, in situations where the publisher prints the book and sells to the club at heavy discounts, the author will be paid a reduced royalty rate for this bulk sale. Both the author and the publisher benefit from additional sales and revenue, while the publisher benefits further from lower unit costs due to bigger print runs. As book club rights are closely tied to other primary rights, these are usually granted and controlled by the publisher, but the author must be informed about such arrangements beforehand and approval sought, though they should not withhold this unreasonably as both stand to benefit. The premise is that book club members are generally additional book buyers and that deals like this increase rather than cannibalize the publisher's regular market.

Book club rights used to be a lucrative subsidiary right, especially in the United Kingdom, some European countries and North America, with deals swiftly concluded on large numbers of popular titles. The traditional book club model has been undergoing an evolution, after cheap deals and swift delivery on e-retail platforms eroded the model. There is now a rise of specialist subscription book boxes, also seen in several African markets, often combined with other products. These are often sold with the backing of online "influencers" or trusted celebrity figures, or publications curating the book offering to subscribers. In Nigeria, publishers have also produced bespoke book club editions for banks or other companies catering to their own corporate book clubs.

4.15.6 Large print rights

Large print rights are granted to and controlled by the publisher, as this is another direct version of the book which could compete if sold separately. Publishers generally sell these rights on rather than producing large print editions themselves, because of specialist skills and separate contacts needed, usually with libraries. Where a license is sold, the split ranges between 50 percent and 60 percent for the author. Where finished copies are sold, the royalty is approximately 10 percent or lower as these are sold in very small quantities and have high unit costs.

Large print rights deals are becoming less common as e-book reading offers font adjustment options for those who can read digitally. There is, however, still demand for large print deals in actual print and bound editions, especially for libraries, for those not comfortable with e-book reading, those not able to access e-book reading devices or those without access to reliable power supply, broadband or e-book retailers.

4.15.7 Free license for visually impaired person access

There is also a separate clause allowing the publisher to license, for free, the transfer or recording of the work in Braille or audio for non-commercial use for visually impaired persons only. The Marrakesh VIP Treaty of 2013[15] has been ratified by many international publishers, allowing for copyright exceptions to facilitate the creation of accessible versions of books and other copyrighted works for visually impaired persons. Note that use under Marrakesh exceptions is in many countries not remunerated and as such no royalties will be payable. This

15 Formally the Marrakesh Treaty to Facilitate Access to Published Works for Persons who are Blind, Visually Impaired or Otherwise Print Disabled, colloquially known as the Marrakesh Treaty.

is also the case in territories where a publisher may be required by law to produce such formats, as long as the publisher is not remunerated for such work. Only in some countries is a fee managed by CMOs (for example, in Germany).

4.15.8 Condensation rights

Some companies with regularly subscribing readers may want to buy rights to many publications and condense (or "digest") the works into easier, swifter reading for their members. They then pay a condensation rights fee to authors who are included in a "condensed book" volume. Where an originating publisher operates in the condensed book publishers' market, these deals are usually done via the publisher, as these editions are seen to offer some competition to the original edition the publisher has produced. Publishers are unlikely to sign up a work where they do not have condensation rights. However, in some translation markets a condensed edition has been known to precede and stimulate a full-length volume deal. It is crucial that the author is consulted and gives their consent to this subsidiary right beforehand. Condensation involves shortening and changes to the author's work for the purpose of inclusion in a bound multi-author condensed book volume, and as such requires a moral rights waiver. Authors are generally not given approval over the final digested text in these instances, hence the waiver.

4.15.9 Anthology rights and permissions

An author's work may be included in volumes such as poetry, short story and essay anthologies, or other compilations of work from different sources. These anthology rights are usually part of the package of rights granted to the publisher by the author. In addition to the fee offered, the publisher and the author must consider the reputation of the anthology and its editor and the other works that are included, and whether the authors want their work and name to be associated with the anthology or compilation. The compensation to the publisher and author often depends on the size of their contribution to the anthology, as well as the status of the author. Sometimes this is a small percentage of the royalties or a one-off payment, often with a proviso for further payment due on subsequent print runs or editions.

Though there is some overlap, permissions involve the use of smaller amounts of material from the original work, such as:

- lines of poems as epigraphs for books or other poems;
- lines quoted in novels and biographies; or
- maps, illustrations, graphs and tables in textbooks or other publications.

Permissions may include sections of text, full chapters or graphs, photos and illustrations from original works. This also includes the use of individual poems and short stories in anthologies or in textbooks for illustrations or exercises like comprehension practice. The payment is usually determined by the amount of material used in the other publication as a fraction of the total publication and also the type of work quoted. Poetry, for example, by its concise nature, generally attracts a higher rate per word than prose. The fame of the author and the popularity of the work are also factors in permission fees, as are the extent of the territory, the number of printed copies and the number of times the book is reprinted. Permission fees may be relatively small amounts individually, but can add up, especially over the in-copyright span of a popular work.

Permissions are usually part of the rights granted to the publisher and as such are administered by the publisher, though authors with concerns about how their work is used or quoted may make different arrangements and prefer an agent to handle this. Due to the small amounts involved and the frequency of requests for usage of the material, the author is not always consulted by the publisher, unless this is contractually stipulated. Depending on whether the permission is for a small quotation or more material, permissions may be granted for free, but should include at least one free copy for the author. The publisher is obliged to account to the author on permission usage of their work when they report on royalties.

As covered in Sections 4.4 and 4.6 regarding the author's warranties and the delivery clause respectively, authors of new works must understand that they will need to get permission to use other publishers' and authors' copyright content.

The long-standing permissions regimes around the world demonstrate that there is always a viable licensing solution for the use of authors' IP, as opposed to large-scale use of copyright material hosted on pirate sites, or illicit TDM and "scraping" for machine learning, as is the case with ongoing copyright infringements by many tech companies in the development of generative AI. In some countries and regions there have been campaigns for the possibility of a TDM exception, but in several territories there have been counter-campaigns and legal conclusions that such "scraping" for LLMs is not to be covered by a TDM exception. The principle of copyright and authors' rights remains such that authors must be consulted and must give approval for the use of their copyright work, licensed according to whatever appropriate terms can be agreed.

4.15.10 Educational editions

The author's work may be licensed for educational purposes in different ways, such as extracts being included in textbooks via the permissions route described above, in which the consent of the author is required for each extract or use. The author's work may also be incorporated in educational games and accompanying digital assets that are used for learning purposes. While a different licensing fee will be determined for these, the use of content for the development of videos can overlap with film and performance rights and care must be taken around the holistic management of all the author's rights to avoid conflict.

This section is concerned with the development of a single-author educational edition. This is when a publisher commissions an educational adaptation of an existing work (such as a novel) for a school readership, with introduction and extra learning materials added. If there is textual adaptation, this should always require author approval. The split on an educational edition, while being no less than equal shares, may depend on whether the author is required to do additional work with regard to ancillary material and reading and approving the edition. Where educational editions are prescribed by large educational authorities, such an edition might provide a valuable source of additional income.

In addition to full single-author editions, licenses may be required in order for users to make copies of sections of published material for inclusion in course packs or in hand-outs for distribution to learners in a class, in both print and digital formats. These are negotiated by a CMO, licensing agency or reproduction rights organization (RRO) with a university or school administration. CMOS and RROs are covered in more detail under the collective licensing section below.

- stating who is responsible for supplying metadata about the publication to the RRO (usually the publisher); and
- whether the publisher is responsible for collecting the fees and paying over the author's share in a timely fashion and according to the contract.

Remuneration from RROs may not be recoupable from the advance paid to the author in all territories, so do check the legal situation in your jurisdiction.

4.15.11 Merchandizing

In specific areas of publishing, such as children's books, merchandizing rights may refer to the licensing of a character or design into a different medium, often a series of linked products featuring fictional characters. This could include stationery, costumes and soft toys to tie in with children's books, science-fiction and fantasy series, or graphic novels. One book or series can produce many separate merchandizing deals for different products with different manufacturers, according to their specific product expertise. Merchandizing rights are also generally strictly limited for a period and for particular territories, where consumers will have different preferences and buying patterns. This is a complex commercial area, which involves pitching to and negotiating with a wide range of potential suppliers. The production and sale of merchandise is vulnerable to piracy and copyright theft. Very few books will attract serious merchandizing interest; a film or television series deal will often be the trigger for activity in this area. As with film and television rights, merchandizing rights are most often managed by agents or other merchandizing specialists.

4.15.12 Audio

As mentioned above, audio rights are sometimes granted to the publisher and sometimes retained by the author. This depends on the extent of the independent audiobook market, negotiation power, contractual situations and the publishers' capacity to produce audio themselves. There would usually be attendant clauses around the publisher's commitment to publish in this format or to sell rights on in a timely fashion, otherwise to revert on or close to publication date. Unabridged audio remains the more usual format these days, given digital technology, but publishers might still acquire the right to produce abridged audio (though this was more common in the past). An abridged edition would require a moral rights waiver or authorization by the author.

The author would also have narrator approval or meaningful consultation around the choice of narrator. A separate narrator contract and fee is required if the author also narrates their own work for audio. Unlike the main book contract this would involve a flat fee for recording work done and there would be no further royalties beyond the main audio royalty in the contract.

Should an author wish to narrate their own book, the final decision would usually rest with the publisher. However, the author should be taken into serious consideration. Narrators should ensure that the narration contract forbids the use of their voice recordings for AI voice cloning. Such clauses are becoming increasingly important to guarantee the future of human performance in publishing and authorship, since individual voice recordings can be "scraped," or extracted, by companies outside the publisher's business and rights territory.

4.15.13 Radio

Radio rights in a book contract can refer to two quite different formats for broadcasting on radio. With straight reading rights, a whole book is usually read in several installments of slightly adapted parts. Radio adaptation rights are more akin to film, television and theater rights as they involve dramatic adaptation of the book and a separate script with voice actors. With both formats, the author and publisher must be careful that there is no overlap or duplication of audiovisual rights granted to different parties. This also applies to the rise of formats such as podcasting and multi-voice audio: it is essential that there is clarity regarding the detail of all non-print format contracts in this rapidly changing field, to avoid contractual conflict and overlap and the loss of commercial opportunities. Unlike the full reading or adaptation of a book, reading rights of extracts from books may sometimes be managed through CMOs or RROs.

4.15.14 Film, television and theater rights

While for many novelists the idea of a film or television series being made from their work would be a dream come true, this dream is not often realized. Books can be optioned by producers many times before a film version reaches viewers' screens. In developed publishing markets, film and television, theater and other dramatic rights can sometimes be retained by authors and sold directly or via agents. In some markets authors may find themselves under pressure to concede these rights alongside publishing rights, especially with the proliferation of producers seeking IP for streaming content.

Considerations as to whether allied rights like radio and film and television are granted in a publishing contract include a publisher's size and capacity, the author's position and the size of the offer. Film agenting represents a complex and specialized field, including the recent developments in film and television streaming, and requires close cooperation with authors over many years of optioning, re-optioning, adaptation and development. For this reason, contract negotiation in this area is often best left to specialist screen agents.

In some countries (France or Germany, for example), it is mandatory for the audiovisual rights to be included in a separate contract from the publishing agreement. In practice, this may often result in the author signing two contracts with the publisher for both sets of rights, as publishers will seek to acquire audiovisual rights. However, it should be possible for the author to retain these rights and sign directly with the producer.

Some of the following numbered points reference scenarios more relevant to academic and educational publishing rather than trade publishing contracts for general books.

4.15.15 Rental and lending rights

Recently, especially for academic and professional books, book rentals and lending systems have arisen as new revenue streams.

Here, users opt to rent textbooks instead of owning their own copies. The book rental may be in the form of a digital license for a period or the rental of a physical copy. The price of using such books via rental is usually lower than the price of the actual or digital copy. These rights compete with the traditional exploitation of the work, therefore, the publisher must license these rights from the author and ensure details are agreed and appropriately recorded in the contract, specifying the percentage of the total fees that will accrue to the author. Where contracts do not already provide for this exploitation, the publisher must negotiate with the author and agree on the fees for the author, in the form of an addendum. The new concept of book rental can result in complex accounting system requirements, which must be clearly explained and agreed to with the author, who must give consent to this usage.

On the other hand, the lending of publications (through CMOs or RROs in some countries or regions) is governed by the law (for example, PLR in Denmark, Norway, Sweden, New Zealand, Canada, the UK and many European countries). In some jurisdictions, this is an exclusive legal right for the author. It is designed to compensate the author for the loss of income through free lending of their work via libraries. While the management of PLR of print copies has been straightforward with regard to compensation of rights holders, digital lending is not always covered within these schemes, though in many countries (including the UK) e-books and audiobooks are also included and illustrators, translators and audiobook narrators are also eligible for a share of PLR. Some publishers may nevertheless choose not to make electronic books available to libraries, partly to safeguard the electronic markets and to protect the author's rights and the publisher's investments. In some contracts digital lending rights are governed under volunteer licensing and agreements should indicate the consent of the author for electronic lending, and that the publisher has the right to exercise the e-lending right. It should also state what accrues to the author. Where lending is governed by law, and payments are made through a central body, not via publishers (as is the case in many jurisdictions), the publisher must ensure that their agreement with the author complies with the law. Further information on PLR can be found on the WIPO website.[16]

Text and data mining (TDM) rights

Many regions are reviewing copyright law and exception proposals on TDM rights, especially in view of computer-generated works (CGW) and the rising use of AI. The general practice in many regions includes exceptions for TDM for non-commercial scientific research. The difficulty with TDM even where it is for non-commercial and scientific research is that some of its activities (including downloading of copyright materials, the creation of new data sets and reformatting) infringe on the exclusive rights of rights holders. If works are scraped without licensing and used in unsupervised machine learning and competitive products are produced via generative AI, this is not only illegal and harms the author's income but also damages the investments of publishers. It can be asserted that machine learning represents a new type of use (not covered by TDM). Therefore, authors and publishers are now being encouraged to ensure that opt-out language forbidding TDM is formulated in contracts and opt-out language is also included in electronic and print versions of the work, for instance, in accordance with the standards of an ISCC (International Standard Content Code) identifier within the metadata and imprint. For clarity such language should also be included in the terms and conditions on publishers' and authors' websites. Further developments will show whether the new practice of machine learning opens up new licensing models, for which rightly the author will need to give explicit consent.

---

16 https://www.wipo.int/wipo_magazine/en/2018/03/article_0007.html

4.15.16 Online database rights

Online database rights and CD-ROM optical disk rights are mainly of relevance to reference, educational and academic publishing and would not feature in general trade publishing contracts. Databases are protected by copyright law, in the same way as a literary work or computer program, as long as they are original and exist in a material form. This is irrespective of the fact that its content may be made up of non-infringing or publicly available material. It is the compilation, the presentation and the data management system that is protected. The copyright to the database belongs to the compiler. Companies tend to buy the databases outright from the compilers and copyright holders, either with a maintenance and updating arrangement or an agreement to do this themselves. Copyright ownership and assignment with databases is complex and usually depends on the negotiations and agreements reached. It is important that compilers understand their contribution to the compilation, its value, the operating system and their involvement in the future in order to get a fair price for their work. They must also make a considered decision as to whether the license is exclusive or non-exclusive. In some situations, the licensee may want to license other users to the database for further earnings and in that case the licensor may want to earn a royalty on future earnings or be compensated adequately. In other situations the database may be acquired only for the licensee's one-off internal use, such as building up marketing contacts.

4.15.17 CD-ROM optical disk rights

CD-ROM rights are part of the optical disk rights (which would include CDs, DVDs and Blu-Ray disks). The format most commonly used in the academic book sector (and also sometimes in children's books) is CD-ROM. Although this is fairly old technology, CD-ROM rights were bundled together in earlier contracts as part of e-rights or referred to as part of future technology rights, or even the vague "unknown usage" (wording to be avoided by authors). There have been several disputes about CD-ROM and other e-rights between publishers and authors on whether the publisher has the right to include the published materials on CD-ROM. As with all future exploitations, it is important that the publisher and the author agree on these rights and also that when the time comes for the publisher to distribute the content on CD-ROM, the author is notified and grants consent.

Distributing the published materials by means of CD-ROM and other devices and on electronic platforms can broaden the use of the materials. A major complication with CD-ROM and e-platforms is that they include many different individual works, compiled and arranged by the publisher, and it can become difficult to determine the contribution of the individual author to the full CD-ROM or platform. While CD-ROMs are static and usage of each contributor's material cannot be determined, with platforms there is sophisticated software that can monitor and report on the usage of each contributor's material to determine compensation. One of the biggest challenges of determining CD-ROM compilation compensation to participating authors is a consideration of what authors earned when their materials were standalone versus when they were included in the compilation. Due to their popularity as standalones, some such authors may end up receiving less than they were getting as standalones while others who were getting less begin to get more, by being placed alongside other reputable authors' work. All these variables must be considered in determining individual compensation.

4.15.18 Digital technology, learning tools and publisher-owned content

As in the compilation of databases and CD-ROMs covered above, more publishers are developing learning tools that include other learning aids and functions, including:

- diagnostics;
- interactive media;
- assessment and remedial functions;
- digital assets; and
- traditional text and illustrations.

Such tools are driven by sophisticated learning software or AI. The tool is made up of different copyright materials, including text, digital assets and software. Compared to traditional textbook contracts, these digital learning tools can pose a significant challenge for the administration of copyright. Many education publishers are reverting to developing, buying and owning all the components that make up the learning tool. This gives them the flexibility to respond to curriculum changes and requirements, build appropriate learning tools and avoid negotiations with different rights holders for different components. In doing so, publishers must comply with national legislation. Some countries are developing legislation where writers have to give consent, and have the right to benefit from all future exploitation of their work, including scraping and machine learning. In other countries, this is not the case, for example, when TDM is not subject to a lawful opt-out mechanism, or to remuneration. One example is Japan, where authors or translators cannot restrict the usage of their works due to the national law. This is where issues like functioning opt-out mechanisms come into play. These also concern publishers if they want to avoid, for example, their e-books being bundled into repositories and "mined" for commercial purposes without remuneration or even information to the author. Authors who are commissioned to develop such material need to understand the full context of the future exploitation of their work and their relative contribution to the learning toolkit, in order to negotiate fair one-off compensation.

With digital uses in particular, some publishers may want to try to secure rights for as yet "unknown usages." As mentioned earlier, it is important that authors only expressly agree to tried-and-tested rights that are explicitly mentioned in the contract.

AI training uses?[17]

The Authors Guild has drafted a new model clause to prohibit the use of an author's work for training artificial intelligence technologies without the author's express permission. [...] Authors should be on the lookout for clauses that allow their work to be used for AI training, which involves copying the work many times over. Such clauses sometimes refer to AI expressly, but other times they are more oblique, giving a publisher or distributor the right to use an author's work for "internal purposes," "research," or "data mining."
[...]
The model clause is below:

No generative AI training use

For avoidance of doubt, Author reserves the rights, and [Publisher/Platform] has no rights to, reproduce and/or otherwise use the Work in any manner for purposes of training artificial intelligence technologies to generate text, including without limitation, technologies that are capable of generating works in the same style or genre as the Work, unless [Publisher/Platform] obtains Author's specific and express permission to do so. Nor does [Publisher/Platform] have the right to sublicense others to reproduce and/or otherwise use the Work in any manner for purposes of training artificial intelligence technologies to generate text without Author's specific and express permission.

4.15.19 Collective licensing

As noted earlier, in some circumstances, the contract should include a clause about collective licensing. Collective licensing is a rights management system where an organization (such as a CMO or RRO, mentioned under educational editions above) collects fees on behalf of rights holders for specific use. This is often done by schools and universities, but also for other purposes such as use in a radio broadcast or article where the author was not contacted directly. An RRO usually keeps a percentage to cover their administration costs and disburses the rest to the authors and, in some countries, to other rights holders.

In these licenses, payment is determined by the amount of the work used, the number of students and the number of copies required. Educational use may sometimes compete with original textbook material, but where there is a reluctance or inability for students to buy the whole book this may be the only income that is received from the educational institution. If the

17 The content of this case study is taken directly from The Authors Guild website: https://authorsguild.org/news/model-clause-prohibiting-ai-training/#:~:text=For%20avoidance%20of%20doubt%2C%20Author,generating%20works%20in%20the%20same

material is from a non-textbook work, this is welcome additional income for the author and publisher.

RROs have two methods of licensing for educational use of published materials. The most common method is called blanket licensing in which a university or school gets a general license to use the materials of authors and publishers that are included in the agreement with the RRO. They pay a fixed annual fee for all their usage. The RRO distributes the amount among the participating authors and publishers. The other, less common, licensing approach is transactional licensing where the institution uses the materials, records what they have used and pays the RRO accordingly. The RRO then distributes to the publishers along with the transaction report. Due to the amount of administrative work involved in transactional licensing, educational institutions often prefer the less cumbersome blanket licensing.

In some countries, legislation supports the operation of RROs by enabling schools and universities to copy works through a compensated exception or an extended collective license. RROs are usually governed by national laws to ensure good governance and proper disbursement of collections to members. Information about these different national approaches can be found on the IFRRO website.

The main approaches are voluntary licensing, systems with support mechanisms for collective licensing (such as extended collective licensing), legal licensing and levy remuneration. Further information about each of these systems is available from IFRRO,[18] and in the WIPO publication, Collective Management of Text and Image-Based Works.[19]

RROs also have an international network, so that the works represented by one RRO are also represented by RROs in other countries. These networks also ensure that payments made for copying under RRO licenses in other countries are exchanged between RROs and paid to the mandating rightsholders.

For the purposes of this publication, it is important for authors and publishers to be aware of the system operating in their countries and, if necessary, include provisions regarding collective management in the contract. These provisions might include:

- deciding on the appropriate share of fees between the author and publisher (although some countries decide, through legislation, what the splits between authors or publishers should be, or if publishers are getting a share at all;
- stating who is responsible for supplying metadata about the publication to the RRO (usually the publisher, if they are receiving a share) and;
- whether the publisher is responsible for collecting the fees and paying over the author's share in a timely fashion and according to the contract.

Remuneration from RROs may not be recoupable from the advance paid to the author in all territories, so do check the legal situation in your jurisdiction.

The mandate to the RRO is not exclusive. Publishers and authors can still license the use of their content by educational institutions and other users directly and in competition with the RRO. Authors may also have many works which will qualify for income from RROs, outside of the works licensed in book form to publishers, so it is important for authors to register all their works with RROs.

In some countries, the receipt and distribution of PLR income should also be covered in the contract. In some countries, publishers are eligible to receive PLR payments; in others the payments are made only to authors. In any event, as with registering for collective licensing systems, authors should be aware of the importance of registering for PLR as it can be an important supplemental source of income. Further information is available on the PLR International website.[20]

18 IFRRO: International Federation of Reproduction Rights Organisations, https://ifrro.org/
19 World Intellectual Property Organization, 2022. *Collective Management of Text and Image-Based Works*. Geneva: WIPO. www.wipo.int/publications/en/details.jsp?id=4664
20 https://plrinternational.com/

4.15.20 Supply of subsidiary agreements

The author will have the right of approval on specified subsidiary rights in the contract before they are granted to third parties. It is essential for the publisher to keep the author fully informed and ask for the necessary written consent regarding where secondary rights to their work are granted around the world, and on what terms. The contract should include a clause about the arrangement regarding supply of agreements to the author, either direct or via the agent, within a certain period from the date of agreement. The author and their agent or financial advisor will need to see and record all the details of the subsidiary rights agreements in order to check royalty statements and payments accurately. Like royalties, subsidiary rights income will contribute to the author's advance earn-out.

4.16 Film quit claim

Producers and film and television companies acquiring screen adaptation rights to books must be sure no one else has a claim on those rights. They will also insist on the right to use extracts or plot summaries of the book for advertising and sales purposes. They will ask the author to secure these confirmations in writing from the publisher at the time of the adaptation deal. It is therefore best to agree such wording between author and publisher at initial publishing contract stage, to ensure smooth progress later. This clause confirms that the publisher does not have film rights and includes a limit on the use of the text by the film company, so as not to encroach on publishing rights. For instance, this limit could be 10,000 words or, if the work is short, a smaller amount like 7,500 words.

4.17 Accounting: statements, payments, examination and remedies

4.17.1 Statements and payments

This clause sets how the publisher should report on the work's sales to the author, ideally on a twice-yearly basis (or "bi-annually") or sometimes annually. While accounting dates differ in some markets, there may be a three-month period between the end of the term over which sales have been made and accounted for, and the delivery of relevant statements and any resulting payment to the author (or their agent, as provided for in the contract). This clause will state that clear statements will be provided even when no money is due. A provision will be made for interest being payable on late payment.

There are significant challenges in some emerging markets which lack reliable sales data and retail statistics for comparison and context. The author (and their agent) need to ensure that the publisher has the capacity to track and report sales clearly. Some contracts make clear stipulation of exactly what royalty statements should show. For example, accounts may state:

- the title, ISBNs and various formats of the work;
- the publication date;
- the number of the initial print;
- the number of copies in stock, if any, at the beginning of the accounting period;
- the number of copies printed, if any, during the accounting period;
- the number of copies presented free of charge during the accounting period (for the purposes of promotion, endorsement and media);
- the number of copies remaining in stock at the end of the accounting period;
- the cumulative sales of the work since publication;
- the published price of the work since publication;
- the royalty rate payable;
- the advance payment to be recouped (if applicable);
- the total payment due to the author;
- the percentage of the hold-back provision made in case of returned books (the "reserve against returns");
- the number of copies, if any, sold off or remaindered during the period; and
- all revenues from licensing (e.g., serial, translation and other rights).

As electronic distribution increases, it is also necessary to determine the exact number of titles sold via these channels. Transparency can be difficult with commercial flat-rate models. In principle, however, the author and the publisher have the right to be able to track the use of their joint work.

4.17.2 Examination and remedies

This clause seeks to provide procedures and remedies for accounting disputes which can occur between the author and the publisher. If the author is not satisfied with and contests the statement of account on their royalties or fees, the clause enables the author or their representatives to inspect the publisher's accounts. To avoid frivolous and costly challenges and negligence on the publishers' side, the cost of the review accrues to either the author or the publisher. Often, if the statements are found to be erroneous by more than 10 percent, the publisher is required to rectify at their cost. If the discrepancy turns out to be less than 10 percent, the author is required to carry the cost of the review. The clause fosters due diligence by both parties to avoid unnecessary costs.

4.17.3 Tax note

There would generally be a short clause to explain that all payments, royalties and percentages set out in the agreement are exclusive of any value added tax (VAT) or general sales tax (GST). These taxes must be added by the publisher, if required, according to the statutory regulations and the status of the author. This depends on whether they are entitled to collect and pass on VAT (for book products or copyrighted works).

4.18 Author's copies

The clause states the number of copies that are given to the author (and their agent, if relevant) for free. These copies are for the author's use, including for their own archives or giving away to friends and colleagues. This is usually a limited number, depending on the number of printed copies, format and cost of individual books. Quantities can vary and are usually negotiable. This is in addition to copies that the author may request for additional promotional activities, as coordinated with the publisher. There should also be a provision for discounted copies for the author's own use, not generally for resale. To be fair, the discount should be equal to or more favorable to the author than the trade discounts the publisher offers. Some authors such as children's authors or poets may, by agreement with the publisher, sell their own books at readings or school events where there is no bookseller present.

There should also be a provision for the author to receive some free bound proof copies, if these are produced, as well as a smaller number of copies for all subsidiary rights and subsequent editions, including a free audio or e-book download.

4.19 Termination: publication cessation, rate of sale, remainders

Some books will go on selling well beyond the author's life, but for others demand may cease after a few years. This clause allows for the termination of the agreement and the reversion of the rights to the author if sales of the author's book have ceased or slowed substantially. Initially, if a publisher needs to reduce stock that is not selling in order to make warehouse space, they may remainder some print copies but keep the print edition available. Sometimes the publisher may choose to dispose of excess copies at the best possible offer price. They are obliged by a clause in the contract to inform the author beforehand and offer them the chance to buy remainder copies at cost. The contract must also specify the royalty arrangement with such copies. Usually there are no royalties payable to the author if the copies are sold at a price below cost or are sold to the author at a considerable discount. In some countries (such as France, Germany and Nordic countries), this has been challenged as authors ask for their remuneration even if the price of the book has been lowered to allow the publisher to sell off the remaining stock.

If the publisher notes that demand for the work has ceased entirely or they decide they can no longer sustain the continuation of the print publication, they are required to inform the author.

A termination clause for cessation of sale should provide a definition of "out of print" or "out of commerce." This can no longer simply depend on whether physical copies exist in a warehouse. Instead it requires active sales and usually an appropriate agreed "rate-of-sale" threshold, depending on the market and genre of the book. If the main edition sales fall below this threshold over the last one or two accounting periods, the author may request a reversion. There may be a period in which the publisher can respond, reprint or revive sales, before all rights terminate. Valid existing sublicenses would be allowed to continue for their specified agreed term even as the rights to the main edition revert, unless otherwise agreed. Reversion clauses will vary, dependent on negotiations, as to whether e-books will be included in rate-of-sale provisions or not. Authors would generally request to revert rights if an e-book is the only edition available, unless they had specifically entered an agreement for an e-book first, or e-book only edition.

Various administrative details must be clearly defined in such an event, for example, what happens to the production materials, including the setting of the document, film and remaining copies. In many jurisdictions, publishers have rights over final layout and design of the text files. They may insist on being compensated for these by the author or whoever takes on the work, if this layout and design is used and the new publisher is not re-setting the text. This clause should state exactly how the reversion will happen, for instance, the determination of the price of the files and other production material and the price for remaining stock. The author is then free to continue exploiting this work on their own or to find another publisher.

In the event of the reversion of rights to the author, the production materials, including typescript materials and digital files, should be transferred to the author on request (in addition to the unsold copies). The author must think carefully about what they want to do with these before making an offer to purchase these materials. For example, if the author is only interested in continuing the publication in digital format or online, there is no need to buy the print files, and text can be re-set.

Note that in some jurisdictions the reversion of rights is governed by law and as such parties to the agreement must comply with the law.

4.20 Termination: bankruptcy or liquidation

The bankruptcy or liquidation clause stipulates that, upon the liquidation of the publishing company due to bankruptcy or any other cause, the rights granted to the publisher revert to the author with immediate effect. In some countries, such as France, this is now an obligation under a recent law passed concerning liquidations. It is important to note that in some jurisdictions, as mentioned above, the publisher owns and has rights to the final layout and design of the work.

4.21 Copyright infringement

The publisher is responsible for protecting the work from infringement during the term of the agreement with the author. To this end, the publisher places the copyright notice on the imprint page. The notice either states that copyright in the text belongs to the author or that the text belongs to the author and the design to the publisher. Either way, the publisher is responsible for the protection of the work and authorizes the use of the work on behalf of the author during the term of the agreement. The clause in the author's contract allows either party to act against any form of infringement, including seeking damages at their own cost and risk. The parties indemnify each other from the risk that may arise from litigation.

Despite the provisions of the agreement, it is good practice for the publisher, with their institutional capacity, to protect the work and prosecute infringement where they see it as viable. It is also important for the author to lend support to the publisher's effort to protect the work and seek damages where necessary. Such collaboration protects the interests of both parties and makes the process more manageable. It is essential that the publisher notifies the author of the infringement and their plans to have the matter pursued.

Depending on the scale and frequency of the infringement, detailed investigation and successful prosecution is not always possible, especially in the digital environment where infringement may be ongoing. Copyright infringement in some territories has become so rampant, especially regarding digital materials, that authors' and publishers' associations need to work together with law enforcement to counter the practice. Focusing on individual cases and titles may not be cost effective. Recent developments around generative AI underline the challenges here too.

4.22 Force majeure

To protect both parties against developments beyond their control, a force majeure clause is required. This includes natural disasters, like floods and earthquakes, or pandemics and other forces that no one can be held accountable for. The force majeure clause protects both parties from penalties for failing to meet obligations as a result of such events. Such natural forces may prevent the author from delivering the manuscript on the due date or the publisher from publishing the book on the agreed day. The clause should not be open-ended but should specify the period in which both parties must meet their obligations to each other after the event, or a reasonable or renegotiated time to do so.

The COVID-19 pandemic is a recent circumstance where force majeure could be applicable in some cases. Many authors, publishers and other players in the value chain could not meet their obligations due to statutory lockdowns, illness, bereavement or shortfall of human resources that resulted from COVID-19. Many parties had to revisit their arrangements and delivery dates to accommodate this. As with several other clauses already covered, the force majeure clause is a provision of last resort, but nothing trumps good faith between parties in their negotiations in order to overcome unfortunate events. In a well-managed relationship between parties this clause should not need to be invoked, as parties can always review these obligations in good faith and seek to make alternative arrangements and accommodations to mutual benefit.

4.23 Disputes and interpretation

Even with relationships that are extremely congenial at the outset, problems and disagreements can arise, often where one party fails to meet contractual obligations to the other. Contracts may contain a clause delineating the dispute resolution mechanisms if there is any disagreement around the meaning or interpretation of the contract's clauses. This clause may suggest reference to arbitration, depending on the jurisdiction. Arbitration can, however, be very expensive and time-consuming, and often matters that are subject to arbitration still end up in court. Sometimes appropriate small claims courts may be a good option for such disputes. Contracts may omit mention of arbitration or an "interpretation and disputes" clause entirely, as long as there is reference to governing law which the parties will submit to in order to settle disputes.

4.24 Applicable or governing law

The author and the publisher must agree on the law that will be used to interpret the contract or where the matter will be heard if any dispute goes to court. This clause is straightforward in situations where the author and the publisher are in the same country. The law of that country applies and the courts in the country will hear the case. Disagreement around applicable law generally arises when the author and the publisher are in different countries. Usually, the publisher insists that the laws of the country where they are based will apply. If an agreement cannot be reached on applicable law, the parties can agree to let the courts determine applicable law when the dispute arises.

However, the ideal is to ensure that no disputes are left to escalate to the point of needing to be heard in court. Both parties must try to act in good faith for mutual benefit, to meet obligations to each other and resolve issues through open communication before external intervention is required. In Europe, the recent Mediation Directive suggests parties reach out of court settlements through mediation schemes. But in some jurisdictions mediation schemes may not be available, may be seen to be set up to the benefit of certain interest groups in the sector or may be costly. For many disputes a small claims court track may be an efficient option if all informal avenues have been exhausted.

4.25 Assignment and non-assignment

Authors sign their agreement with one publisher, but the publisher's circumstances and status may change, including in the event of a sale or merger with another company. In some cases, authors may sign a contract with a publisher who is part of a larger group. In this case they may want the assignment to apply to those entities as well. There may also be changes within the group where books may be moved from one imprint to another. The publisher's contract usually tries to cover these situations and developments. However, the author may not want their work associated with another imprint of the publisher. In situations where the company is sold, the contracts become part of the assets that are bought. Again, the publisher's contract seeks to provide for this.

It is important that these situations and developments are negotiated and specified in the contract, including in the preamble. Situations where the whole publishing business is sold to another company are more straightforward as there is a wholesale transfer and the new owner has an obligation to honor the contract and obligations to the author. An individual transfer of the work is usually more problematic and this is where the author may have more ground for objections. Authors may thus prefer to have a clause that requires the publisher to seek their consent before such a transfer. Alternatively, in many cases, there is a mutual arrangement that no party may make such an assignment without the written agreement of the other. The requirement of explicit author consent to transfer of contractual rights in the case of a company takeover appears in some national copyright laws. In a world where corporate consolidations are increasingly frequent, it has been argued that the author should be able to choose to terminate the contract if they are unhappy with their work being under new ownership.

4.26 Option clauses

A publisher who has invested in the development of an author may want to be part of that author's success and future publications. New and independent publishers might be particularly anxious about investing in authors who become successful and then move to larger publishers. But even large, well-established publishers often seek to bind an author contractually to submitting their next work to them exclusively. Some publishers may try to commit an author to submitting work to them and agreeing a deal under the same terms as the current option. This is not a good approach, as it binds the author to what may be a poor contract, but without commitment and input from the publisher to the second book from the start.

A two-book contract, with full commitment and payment obligations, would be a better option to shared risk. And escalating royalties would reward the author for success, being triggered at a stage when it can be sustained by the publisher, having received their income share from the author's work. Bear in mind too that, in some jurisdictions, it is not possible to make a grant of rights on a future work that is not yet in existence.

Overreaching option clauses may prove to be illegal if they try to govern the author's future income using current terms and they can create bad feeling, even without potential legal action. While it is understandable that publishers want to protect their investment in an author and be able to publish their future works, it is better to retain authors and their future work through good service, mutual interest and respect. For authors it is better to negotiate on a work-by-work basis and agree terms that are in line with their current status and the potential of the new work.

Not all contracts will be drafted with option clauses, for the reasons above. If for any reason the author has to sign a contract with an option clause, the language should be closely scrutinized and authors should make sure that it is as limited as possible in terms of the types of works covered. An option clause should be limited to the same genre or series as the first book, and not just state that it is an option to see and offer for "the author's next work." The author should only have to show the publisher a short piece of work (for example, an outline and two chapters) and this should be required as soon as possible after the first book is delivered. The time in which the publisher has to exercise the option should also be kept short, so that the author does not suffer economically with a new work tied up in limbo. In some cases, the publisher is even required to remunerate the option phase monetarily.

4.27 Competing works

In order to protect their investment in the author's work, the publisher may, in exceptional cases, wish to include a "competitive works" or "non-compete" clause. This prohibits the author from developing (or even contributing) to work in the exclusive territory that may be seen to compete with their published work and potentially harm the sales of the published work. Competitive works clauses are often the subject of dispute and from the author's point of view are best avoided. Authors can regard these clauses as one-sided, especially when the publisher may insist on publishing works by other authors that compete with the author's work. It is not in the publisher's interest to harm the sales potential of the work that they have invested in and it is also unproductive for the author to do the same. Most often this understanding is sufficient in practice without a blanket non-compete clause.

Broadly worded competitive works clauses can cause needless economic harm to authors, especially those who are experts in their field. If such a clause has to be included in a contract, wording should refer only to another complete and substantially similar work of the same genre, which would directly and clearly harm sales of the contracted work. The clause should be valid only for a limited time span, which can range from a period after publication of a few months or one year or, if need be, a maximum of two years.

4.28 Agency clause

If the author has an agent, there should be a clause stating that the author has appointed an agent representative who is empowered to act on the author's behalf and to potentially receive payments which they will pass on after subtracting their commission. There will be wording to allow for direct payment to the author and the agent separately, should the author and agent part ways. But, unless otherwise negotiated, the agent will remain the agent of record for the contract they negotiated and will be entitled to continue to receive commission on the deal.

4.29 Entire and earlier agreements

Negotiations between the author and the publisher can be protracted. Along the way, many small points of agreement may be reached through various means, including by email and verbally, in person or on the telephone. It is good practice to include the wording "subject to contract" in all correspondence prior to the eventual summarizing deal memo and draft contact. It is important that the agreement that is eventually signed takes into account all these earlier points of agreement, but ultimately supersedes anything that has gone before. The agreement should thus specify that this agreement is recognized as the sole agreement and that there are no other agreements. It also emphasizes that no future agreements or alteration of the agreement will be recognized unless written addenda are signed by both parties. This clause guards against confusion with multiple or earlier agreements, and the involvement of unauthorized persons in issuing other agreements.

4.30 Signature and contract copies

Contracts must be signed before the commencement of the publication process by people that are designated legal representatives of the company, and by the author. They must be initialed, witnessed (if required) and dated properly. They must be signed by both parties and each party must retain a copy for safekeeping. Only when the contracts meet the above-mentioned legal requirements can they be valid. Both the publisher and the author must ensure that these legal requirements are met. With advances in digital document management systems also accelerated by the restrictions of the COVID-19 pandemic, electronic signatures have become more mainstream practice and should be used where possible. However, the publisher should always make available to the author a format of the contract that is printable, readable and modifiable during the contract negotiation process, so it is easy to track changes during the contract editing process.

5 After the contract

The earlier sections have covered the reversion of rights when the demand for the work ceases or declines, and the publisher does not want to continue to publish, or when the author asks for rights to be reverted on the basis of poor performance. We have also discussed what happens when the publishing company is sold or when the work is transferred to another entity. What happens in the event of the author's death?

The author's work remains protected by copyright law for another 50 or 70 years after the author's death, depending on country and national laws, though there is some national variation beyond this too. Copyright will be transferred to the author's estate and successors, as also indicated in the preamble. In the case of an FTOC deal, the publisher will continue to sell the work for the extent of copyright and pay the royalties to the author's estate and heirs. In other cases, the contract ends after the stated terms, for instance, 5, 7 or 10 years. Such contracts may be extended by mutual agreement, whether with the author (who is still alive at the time) or their legal heirs. Sometimes a "refresher" advance payment is made.

The work may also need revisions and updates for new editions, especially in the case of textbooks. Without an author able to make updates, the contract may state that the publisher may recruit suitable contributors to provide the updates. The publisher may deduct the update costs from the amounts that are due to the author's legal heirs or the estate.

Some contracts may allow for certain aspects of the contract, such as royalties for e-book or audio rights, to be revisited and potentially renegotiated if relevant circumstances have changed. These revision clause precedents were introduced to allow flexibility and fairness in areas where technological changes were fast-moving and unpredictable, with a knock-on impact on pricing, publishers' costs and authors' earnings. Some contracts may allow for an overall consideration and good faith renegotiation of terms after a certain period of, say, 1, 2, 5 or 10 years, on request by either party. In other cases, the fixed-term contract will automatically allow the parties to renegotiate, renew or disengage as preferred, after an agreed period.

6 Conclusion

While publishing contracts can seem daunting at first, their logic and shape will become familiar with use, and with practice you will learn to spot omissions or anomalies swiftly. If there is any doubt or confusion about a clause during negotiation it is always worth asking the other party for a clearer explanation: an honest question is often the first step to a mutual resolution and a better contract.

Bear in mind that any amendment to one part of a contract may require amendments elsewhere so as not to create internal contradictions. Careless amendments can often cause confusion and dispute. You will have seen how many parts of a contract work in tandem; the document must be read, considered and understood as a whole before signing. That said, it is possible to return to contracts by mutual agreement to amend terms as necessary through an appropriate addendum. Certain rights may be taken out of the contract or added to it, or territories adapted as the local and international publishing landscape evolves and the parties' own circumstances change.

Good and successful publishing relationships can last a lifetime and build mutual success for both publisher and author. A clear and thorough contract is key, but cannot be a substitute for ongoing commitment to collaboration, fairness and clear and open communication between author and publisher as they seek together to maximize the readership of the work to mutual benefit.

If a good, clear contract is the foundation of a healthy publishing relationship, copyright and authors' rights law is its ultimate bedrock. There are many challenges to copyright and authors' rights – from illegal copying and piracy through to AI and challenges at a legal level in many parts of the world. Publishers, authors and other originators like illustrators and translators must understand the importance of a strong system for safeguarding IP, helping to support individual creators, helping creative sectors to flourish and enriching the lives of global communities. Authors' rights and copyright legislation, education and enforcement remain crucial.

In this vital and dynamic industry and cultural arena there is always much ongoing learning and many good sources of information to draw on. A great deal of knowledge and experience can be gained – and shared – by joining local publishing, bookselling or agents' associations and organizations for writers, translators and visual artists, where they exist in your territory. Further afield, it is helpful to refer to the excellent resources put together by national and international bodies with an interest in supporting the creation and dissemination of quality IP.

Details and links to further resources and IP-focused organizations – by no means an exhaustive list – can be found at the end of this document. This will provide a useful starting point, but will only be the base camp for a fuller, more exciting journey.

Useful links

Copyright information: principles, permissions, piracy and FAQs for authors

Authors Guild (AG) (United States of America) – licensing of copyright
www.authorsguild.org/industry-advocacy/authors-keep-your-copyrights-you-earned-them/

Authors Licensing and Collecting Society (ALCS) – copyright basics for writers
www.alcs.co.uk/copyright-basics-for-writers

Berne Convention – WIPO summary
www.wipo.int/treaties/en/ip/berne/summary_berne.html

British Broadcasting Corporation (BBC) – Copyright Aware
www.bbc.co.uk/copyrightaware

British Copyright Council (BCC) – copyright FAQs
www.britishcopyright.org/wp-content/uploads/BCC-FAQs.pdf

British Copyright Council (BCC) – UK Copyright Highway Code
www.britishcopyright.org/information/category/uk_copyright_highway_code/

Copyright Licensing Agency (CLA)
www.cla.co.uk/

Design and Artists Copyright Society (DACS) – copyright FAQs for visual artists
www.dacs.org.uk/

Get It Right from a Genuine Site
www.getitrightfromagenuinesite.org/genuine-sites

Intellectual Property Office (IPO), UK – guidance for diligent copyright search
www.gov.uk/government/publications/orphan-works-diligent-search-guidance-for-applicants

International Authors Forum (IAF) – Copyright Works
https://internationalauthors.org/wp-content/uploads/2017/10/Copyright-Works.pdf

International Federation of Reproduction Rights Organisations (IFRRO) – video on PLR and how it works in different countries
www.youtube.com/watch?v=wtLCOiW0q6c

PLS Clear
https://plsclear.com/

Société des Auteurs et Compositeurs Dramatiques (SACD) – authors' rights and copyright
www.sacd.fr/en/authors-rights-vs-copyright

Society of Authors (SOA) – guide to copyright and permissions
societyofauthors.org

WATCH (Writers, Artists & Their Copyright Holders)
www.watch-file.com

Other publishing matters

Copyright enforcement news on the IPA website
www.internationalpublishers.org/our-work-menu/copyright-enforcement

IPA INSPIRE report 2022
www.internationalpublishers.org/copyright-news-blog/1209-new-report-building-a-resilient-international-book-sector

Society of Authors, Writers Guild of Great Britain and ALCS Investigation into Contribution Publishing 2021/2022
https://societyofauthors.org/News/News/2021/March/investigation-contribution-publishing
https://societyofauthors.org/News/News/2022/April/Writers-unions-call-for-reform-of-the-%E2%80%98hybrid%E2%80%99

We Need Diverse Books
https://diversebooks.org/

World Kid Lit – resources for publishers of translated children's books
https://worldkidlit.wordpress.com/resources-for-publishers/

International authors', translators' and artists' associations

Alianza Iberoamericana para la Promoción de la Traducción Literaria (ALITRAL)
www.alitral.org/

Members include:
https://abrates.com.br/
https://ace-traductores.org/
www.actti.org/

American Literary Translators Association (ALTA)
www.literarytranslators.org/

Artists Rights Society – United States
https://arsny.com/

Australian Association for Literary Translation (AALITRA)
https://aalitra.org.au/

Authors Guild (AG) – United States
www.authorsguild.org

Design and Artists Copyright Society – United Kingdom
www.dacs.org.uk/

European Writers' Council (EWC)
https://europeanwriterscouncil.eu

International Authors Forum (IAF) – also includes member societies, details and websites
https://internationalauthors.org/

PEN International
www.pen-international.org/

Society of Authors (SOA) - United Kingdom
www2.societyofauthors.org/

Society of Childrens' Book Writers and Illustrators (SCBWI) - international
www.scbwi.org/

Writers' Guild of Great Britain (WGGB)
https://writersguild.org.uk/

Writers' Union of Canada (TWUC)
www.writersunion.ca/

International publishing organizations and associations

African Publishers Network (APNET)
https://apnetafrica.org/

Arab Publishers Association (APA)
www.arab-pa.org/Ar/StaticPages/HomeAr.aspx

Federation of European Publishers (FEP)
https://fep-fee.eu/

Independent Publishers Guild (IPG) - United Kingdom
www.independentpublishersguild.com

International Board on Books for Young People (IBBY)
www.ibby.org/

International Publishers Association (IPA)
www.internationalpublishers.org/

Publishers Association (PA) - United Kingdom
www.publishers.org.uk/

Publishers Association of New Zealand (PANZ)
https://publishers.org.nz/

Publishers' Association of South Africa (PASA)
https://publishsa.co.za/

Publishing Ireland
www.publishingireland.com/

Publishing Scotland
www.publishingscotland.org/

International agents' associations

Association of American Literary Agents (AALA) - United States
https://aalitagents.org/

Association of Authors' Agents (AAA) - United Kingdom
www.agentsassoc.co.uk/

Australian Literary Agents' Association
www.austlitagentsassoc.com/

Copyright, IP, PLR, collective licensing and related organizations

International Federation of Reproduction Rights Organisations (IFRRO)
https://ifrro.org/

More on international PLR and international members:
https://ifrro.org/page/plr/

Public Lending Right (PLR) International
https://plrinternational.com

Further on contractual matters, campaigning, fair terms, model contracts

Alianza Iberoamericana para la Promoción de la Traducción Literaria (ALITRAL) – contract principles
www.alitral.org/p/sobre-contratos.html

Authors' Guild (AG) – model trade book contract
www.authorsguild.org/member-services/legal-services/model-book-contract/

Authors' Guild (AG) – literary translation model contract
www.authorsguild.org/member-services/literary-translation-model-contract/

Authors of Switzerland, Association of German Writers (Austria), Association of German Writers: Charter of Fair Contracts
www.fairerbuchmarkt.de/authors_rights/21.html

European Writers' Council (EWC) – The Value of Writers Work (2014)
https://europeanwriterscouncil.eu/wp-content/uploads/2019/10/EWC_Value-of-Writers-Works_2015.pdf

International Authors Forum – Authors: Ten principles for fair contracts
www.internationalauthors.org/wp-content/uploads/2019/01/Authors-Ten-Principles.pdf
Also available in French and Spanish

International Authors Forum – Visual artists: Ten principles for fair contracts
www.internationalauthors.org/wp-content/uploads/2018/11/Visual-Artists-Ten-Principles.pdf
Also available in French and Spanish

PASA/ANFASA standard contract agreement
https://publishsa.co.za/wp-content/uploads/2021/07/ANFASA-PASA-Agreement-On-Contract-Terms-Apact-2016.pdf

PEN America – A model contract for literary translations
https://pen.org/a-model-contract-for-literary-translations/

Society of Authors (SOA) – CREATOR campaign for fair contracts
www2.societyofauthors.org

Society of Authors (SOA) – Guidance on publishing contracts
www.societyofauthors.org/SOA/MediaLibrary/SOAWebsite/Guides/Guide-to-Publishing-Contracts.pdf

Bibliography and further reading resources

African Publishers' Network (APNET) and Association for the Development of Education in Africa (ADEA) 2000. *African Publishers' Network (APNET)/Association for the Development of Education in Africa (ADEA) Survey*. London: APNET-ADEA.

Blake, C. (1999). *From Pitch to Publication: Everything You Need to Know to Get Your Novel Published.* London: Macmillan.

International Federation of Reproduction Rights Organisations and International Publishers Association (IFRRO-IPA) (2021). *Identifier and Metadata Standards in the Publishing Industry.* Geneva: IFRRO-IPA.
https://ifrro.org/page/article-detail/ifrro-and-ipa-launch-a-report-on-identifier-and-metadata-standards-in-the-publishing-industry/?k=e202110281053428617

Jones, H. and C. Benson. (2016). *Publishing Law.* Abingdon: Routledge.

Owen, L. (ed.) 2006. *Clark's Publishing Agreements: A Book of Precedents*. Seventh Edition. Haywards Heath: Tottel.

Owen, L. (2019). *Selling Rights*. Eighth Edition. Abingdon: Routledge.

Owen, L. (ed.) 2022. *Clark's Publishing Agreements: A Book of Precedents*. Eleventh Edition. London: Bloomsbury.

Stokkmo, O. (2019). *The Role of Collective Licensing*. Geneva: IPA.
https://internationalpublishers.org/licensing-practices-in-a-global-digital-market-the-role-of-cmos/

World Intellectual Property Organization (WIPO) (2007). *Managing Intellectual Property in the Book Publishing Industry: A Business-Oriented Information Booklet*. Geneva: WIPO.

World Intellectual Property Organization (WIPO) (2021). *From Paper to Platform: Publishing, Intellectual Property and the Digital Revolution*. Geneva: WIPO.
www.wipo.int/publications/en/details.jsp?id=4576

World Intellectual Property Organization (WIPO) (2021). *WIPO Good Practice Toolkit for Collective Management Organizations (The Toolkit): A Bridge between Rightholders and Users*. Geneva: WIPO.
www.wipo.int/publications/en/details.jsp?id=4561&plang=EN

World Intellectual Property Organization (WIPO) (2022). *Collective Management of Text and Image-Based Works*. Geneva: WIPO.
www.wipo.int/publications/en/details.jsp?id=4664

www.ingramcontent.com/pod-product-compliance
Lightning Source LLC
Chambersburg PA
CBHW080539240926
51846CB00005BA/947
* 9 7 8 9 2 8 0 5 3 6 2 8 7 *